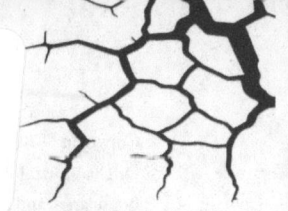

I0418802

A Guide to Navigating Grief, Setting Boundaries, and Finding Strength

Holding without Breaking

How Adult Children Can Support a Grieving Parent Without Losing Themselves

Mischere V. Kyles

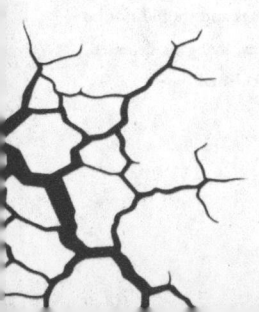

Lineage & Legacy
Publishing

Copyright © 2025 by Mischere V. Kyles, All rights reserved.

Original Title: Holding Without Breaking: A Guide to Navigating Grief, Setting Boundaries, and Finding Strength. How Adult Children Can Support a Grieving Parent Without Losing Themselves.
First edition: October, 2025

No part of this book may be reproduced, stored in a retrieval system, or transmitted in any form or by any means—electronic, mechanical, photocopying, recording, or otherwise—without the prior written permission of the publisher, except in the case of brief quotations embodied in reviews and critical articles.

Published by Lineage & Legacy Publishing
An imprint of Vasiti Enterprises, LLC
Mesa, AZ 85201

ISBN: 979-8-9933843-0-6
Cover design by Mischere V. Kyles
Interior design by Mischere V. Kyles

For permissions or inquiries, contact:
info@mischerekyles.com or http://mischerekyles.com
Printed in the United States of America

Limited Liability & Disclaimer
This book is intended for informational and inspirational purposes only. It is not a substitute for professional counseling, therapy, medical advice, financial guidance, or legal services. Readers are encouraged to seek the support of qualified professionals for matters related to their personal, emotional, financial, or legal circumstances.

Neither the author nor the publisher assumes any responsibility for errors, omissions, or outcomes related to the use of the information contained in this book. By reading this work, you agree that the author and publisher shall not be held liable for any loss, harm, or damages of any kind, whether direct, indirect, incidental, or consequential, arising from the application of the ideas, practices, or examples discussed herein.

All stories and experiences shared are based on personal perspectives and should not be interpreted as universal advice. Any resemblance to actual persons, living or deceased, outside of the author's immediate family experiences, is purely coincidental.

This book carries the spirit of my mother, Delores.
From her life I learned that even after deep loss,
love can still grow—
and strength can be found in the smallest steps forward.

It is for the ones who keep life together
while quietly falling apart inside,
for every adult child who is grieving
while also steadying a parent.

I see your strength.
I feel your love.
I honor the pain you often hide.

Let these pages sit beside you as a steady companion.
May you find here not only comfort,
but reminders that your own healing matters too.

"*To grieve while guiding is a rare strength. To hold others without letting go of yourself—this is the strength that carries love forward.*"

— Mischere V. Kyles

Contents

Preface

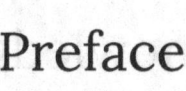
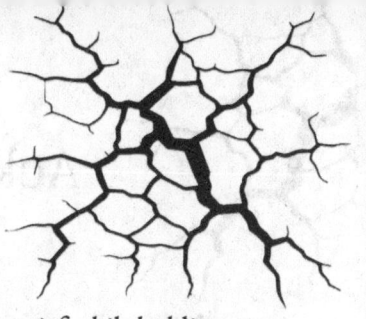

T wice in my life, I've had to carry grief while holding up someone else's world.

The first time, I was a child—watching my mother lose her husband while trying to be the little anchor for my siblings. The second time, I was a grown woman, again standing beside my mother as she faced the impossible. But this time, I carried the weight with adult responsibilities: managing details, making funeral arrangements, comforting others, all while barely making space to feel my own loss.

That experience didn't just crack something open—it revealed something sacred. That there's a hidden strength in being the one others lean on, but also a risk: the quiet erosion of self if you're not careful.

I didn't set out to write this book. I needed this book. And because it didn't exist, I wrote it for you, for every adult child walking this strange road of caregiving, grief, and rediscovery.

May these pages offer a mirror and a balm—a place to rest, to breathe, and to remember that you are not alone.

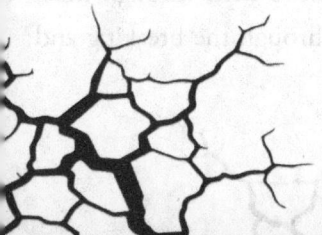

Acknowledgments

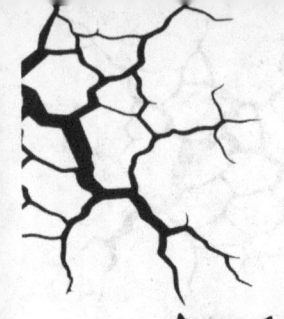

To my family, thank you for your presence, your patience, and the many different yet deeply valuable ways you showed up. You reminded me that love is not one note but a whole chorus, each voice needed in its own way.

To my siblings, thank you for standing with our mother in your own rhythms, for showing that strength wears many forms, and that unity doesn't always look the same, but it always sounds like love.

To my friends, thank you for offering space without pressure, for letting me be both broken and becoming, and for seeing me even when words fell short.

To my GriefShare family, thank you for the sacred gift of community in the middle of heartbreak. Every story, every tear, every quiet nod reminded me that healing happens best when carried together.

To my readers, the adult children learning to hold steady in the storm of loss, this book exists because of you. May it return to you what you've given to others: grace, space, and belonging.

And to God, who gave me the strength to write through tears, memory, and truth. You carried me through the breaking and taught me how to hold.

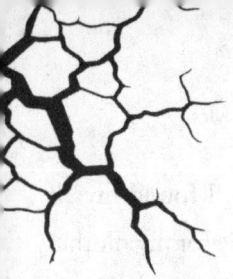

Introduction

One moment, life feels steady. The next, a single phone call, a slammed hospital door, a silence that rings too loud, and suddenly everything you knew splits into before and after.

When a parent dies, the loss doesn't stop with them. The one left behind, the parent who once felt invincible, suddenly looks fragile.And you, their child, are pulled into a role you never expected: the anchor, the helper, the steady one.

Maybe that's you.

The one who answers the late-night calls.
The one who fills the silence at the dinner table.
The one who quietly takes the lead so no one else has to.

I see you.

You are strong
but you are also human.

And carrying both your grief and theirs is heavier than anyone admits.

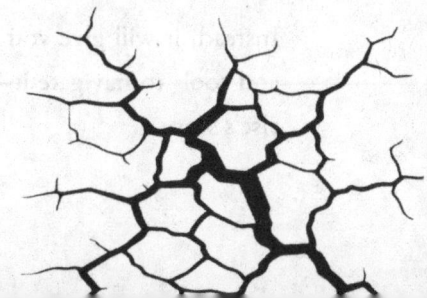

I know this road because I've walked it. Twice, I found myself pulled into the role of the anchor , holding steady for my mother as she navigated devastating loss. Both as a child and as a grown woman, I was left organizing, comforting, and managing the logistics, all while burying my own pain. No one warned me how easy it would be to lose myself in someone else's story, or how heavy it is to carry both your grief and theirs.

This book exists because I needed it, and because it didn't exist. It is for every adult child walking this strange road of caregiving, grief, and rediscovery

A Reader's Promise

If you are holding this book, I imagine you're carrying two weights at once: your own grief and your parent's.

Maybe you're exhausted from being the one everyone leans on.

Maybe you're quietly wondering if you'll break before anyone notices how much you've been holding.

Here's what I want you to know from the beginning: this book will not tell you to "be strong." It will not ask you to ignore your own pain so you can keep functioning for everyone else.

Instead, it will give you language for what you're experiencing and tools to navigate it—without disappearing inside someone else's story.

By the end of these pages, you'll have:

- **Permission** to honor your grief alongside your parent's.
- **Clarity** about boundaries—what's yours to carry and what's not.
- **Anchors** for the overwhelming first weeks when survival feels like the only goal.
- **Perspective** for the long haul, when the doorbells stop ringing but the ache remains.
- **Practical guidance** for both the emotional and everyday realities of loss.

Most importantly, you'll discover that strength is not about holding everything together—it's about knowing what to let go of, while still showing up with love.

What This Book Offers

Think of this book as part memoir, part guide—a steady voice in the storm. A companion that whispers: you matter, too.

Inside, you'll find pieces of my story—raw and unpolished, because grief never is. Alongside them are practices, prompts, and insights to help you honor your parent's grief without abandoning your own.

Every loss looks different. Yet the weight of supporting a grieving parent is something many of us carry in silence. Whether you've lost a father, step-parent, or someone who stood in that role, this book is your space to breathe.

By the end, you'll know how to walk beside your parent in their grief without unraveling in the process. You'll also meet The Four Pillars That Hold You Steady—the truths that carried me when the weight felt unbearable. They'll guide you to:

- **Resist** the urge to do everything, so your parent has room to rebuild their strength.
- **Set** loving boundaries when emotions run high.
- **Honor** your *own* grief without guilt or comparison.
- **Navigate** the practical matters—paperwork, family dynamics, and the dreaded "What now?"

And as you learn these practices, I want you to remember:
You are not selfish for needing space.
You are not invisible, even if no one sees the weight you carry.
You are not alone in holding without breaking.

Because to grieve while guiding is its own strength. And to hold others without letting go of yourself—that is the strength that carries love forward.

That strength begins in the hardest place: the first collision with loss.

How to Use This Book

Grief doesn't move in straight lines. Neither will this book.

You may read it cover to cover, or open to the chapter that meets you where you are right now. Each part offers language for what feels unspeakable and anchors for what feels unsteady:

- **Part One – The Wave and the Weight:** The shock of loss, the busyness that masks grief, and the balance between helping and over-helping.

- **Part Two – The Shifts and the Shadows:** The myth of "time heals," lingering grief, and the cracks that appear in family dynamics.

- **Part Three – The Long Road of Love:** Life after the breaking point—silence, milestones, new roles, and love's quiet lessons.

- **Bonus Chapter – The Four Pillars That Hold You Steady:** Practices to remind you that caring for your parent doesn't mean losing yourself.

This book is both a story and a guide. However you move through it, may it give you steady ground in the middle of the waves.

To deepen your reflection, you can pair this book with the *Holding Without Breaking Companion Journal* and explore additional resources at **www.MischereKyles.com**.

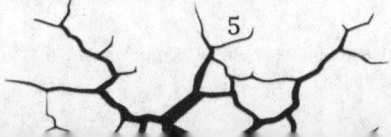

Part I

Illustration by Mischere V. Kyles

The Wave & The Weight

So, let's begin where loss first knocks the wind out of you.

Before you can rebuild, you have to survive the collapse. Before you can steady anyone else, you have to learn what it feels like to stand in the storm yourself.

Grief arrives first as a wave—sudden, crashing, pulling you under before you realize the ground beneath you is gone. The world you knew a moment ago dissolves in saltwater and silence. You come up for air, only to see another swell rising, threatening to drag you back down.

If you've felt that pull already, you know exactly what I mean. Then grief lingers as a weight—quiet, constant, pressing on every breath.

It settles into daily life: the empty chair at the table, the phone calls that never come, the small habits that now echo louder in their absence. Unlike the wave, the weight doesn't announce itself. It simply stays.

I remember when both hit me at once. I was standing in my mother's kitchen, watching her stare at the empty chair where my stepfather used to sit. She didn't say a word, but her silence was louder than anything I'd ever heard. In that moment, I felt the crash of my own grief rising inside me—and at the very same time, the weight of hers settling onto my shoulders.

I wanted to fall apart. But I also knew she was looking to me to hold steady.

That is the complicated truth of being an adult child in grief: you are not just navigating your own storm—you are learning how to steady someone else in theirs. Your parent, the one who once steadied you, now leans into your strength. You love them. You want to help. And yet, beneath that devotion, a quiet question hums:

If I lose myself in their grief, who will carry me?

This first part of the book is about that tension. It weaves story with guidance: how to survive the first wave that knocks your feet out from under you; how to resist the undertow of constant doing; how to loosen your grip when love has turned into fear of letting go; and how to discover that true compassion requires boundaries, not the erasure of self.

The wave will hit. The weight will press. *But you don't have to face them alone.*

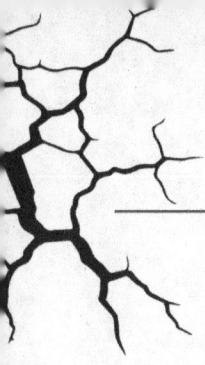

Chapter 1
When the Wave Hits

"Grief is just love with nowhere to go." – Jamie Anderson

Grief doesn't arrive politely.
It doesn't knock.
It doesn't whisper.
It crashes—loud, disorienting, all-consuming—leaving you scrambling for air, reaching for anything solid enough to keep you from going under.

It's the moment you reach for your phone to share a funny story, only to freeze mid-dial.

The empty chair at dinner.

The split second you wake and, for one fragile heartbeat, forget they're gone—until the truth barrels back in like a flood.

And when you're also watching your surviving parent unravel in real time, the water feels deeper. The pull, stronger.

You're not just treading for your own life—you're trying to keep two people afloat in the same storm.

Two currents tugging in opposite directions: theirs, heavy with visible grief; yours, quieter but just as relentless.

9

Some days, you can't tell which current is stronger.

My First Shockwave

I was eleven when it first hit.

We were on a family trip. My siblings, two cousins, and I were in the hotel arcade, riding the sugar high of vacation. Popcorn and soda hung in the air. Tokens clinked into machines. My twin brother and I were locked in an air hockey battle, laughing so loudly adults groaned in mock annoyance.

Then I saw her.

My mother stood in the doorway.

She didn't yell. She didn't even raise her voice.

"*Come upstairs. Now.*"

Her tone was calm, but her face—her face told us everything.

The puck stopped. Tokens slipped from our hands. We followed her in a quiet line, each step heavier, the air thickening like the sky before a storm.

The door between our room and my parents' room stood open. That's when we saw him.

My stepfather lay across the bed, unresponsive. His body jolted as paramedics pressed defibrillator paddles to his chest. The rhythmic beep of the monitor thundered through my head.

Before anyone could stop her, my youngest sister darted forward.

"Daddy!" she screamed.

"No children should be in here!" one of the medics barked.

A hotel staffer pulled her back, closing the door between us. We stood frozen. Listening. Every muffled voice, every footstep on the other side of that door felt like a hammer.

Minutes later, they wheeled him out. We caught only a glimpse—his face pale, wires trailing behind—before he disappeared down the hallway.

We rushed into the car to follow. The siren ahead wailed like a haunting song. In the backseat, we whispered:

"What's happening?"
"Is he okay?"
"Why won't anyone tell us?"

My mother gripped the steering wheel. Her silence was deafening.

At the hospital, antiseptic and anxiety filled the waiting room. I offered to take my sisters to the bathroom—a flimsy excuse to escape the weight of the unknown.

When we returned, the doctor stood in the hallway.

"He didn't make it."

The words hit like a breaker—cold, merciless, filling my lungs with saltwater.

That night, we packed our bags in silence and drove home. No music. No chatter. Just the sound of tires on pavement and the quiet sobs of children who suddenly felt much older.

Our blended family of eight was now seven. His absence left a space no one else could fill.

Home felt wrong. What was supposed to be a summer road trip had ended in silence, the kind that made my head ring. His coffee cup still sat on the counter, a faint brown ring at the bottom. His shoes waited by the door, angled toward the hallway like they expected footsteps. In the bathroom, his aftershave lingered in the air—scent arguing with fact.

Everything looked almost normal, which is what made it unbearable.

Loss doesn't always shout. Sometimes it sits quietly in the places a person once touched.

The Second Shockwave

Years later, my mother remarried. Her new husband was kind, steady, gentle. He didn't try to replace the man we lost, but he became family.

One morning, I got the call.

It had been a peaceful day—hiking with my twin brother, laughing about childhood memories. Later I meditated, grounded, content. The kind of day you want to bottle.

Then my *phone rang*.

It was my aunt. She was with my mom and stepfather on a trip.
"It's not good," she said.
"What's not good?"
"They're trying to revive your stepdad. I called you first. I'll keep you posted."

The line went dead.

I froze. Texted my brother: `Please pray. They're trying to revive Dad.`
In my spirit, I knew. He might not stay.

The second call came.

  "He didn't make it."

The same four words. The same undertow.

I was forty-eight, but the grief hit just as hard. It didn't just reopen old wounds—it deepened them.

I wanted to collapse, but logistics took over:

Who needs to know?
How do we tell my siblings?
What does Mom need?
Funeral arrangements
Paperwork
Flights

No tears. No pause. Just motion.

Underneath it all was a scream I couldn't release. A grief I couldn't stop to feel.

This wave was different. Not because of my age, but because I had to help my mother survive her second devastating loss. Her voice on the phone wasn't frantic—it was fractured. Quiet. Like a cliff edge giving way.

The first time, I was a child forced into adulthood.
The second time, I was grown—but the water somehow felt deeper.

A Warm Memory Before the Call

He asked if I could take the wheel—a rare gesture from a man who almost always drove. Mom slid into the passenger seat while he stretched out in the back, singing along to his favorites from the '70s—Marvin Gaye, Stevie Wonder, the Bee Gees.

Then *Bohemian Rhapsody* came on.

As the first chords filled the car, I caught his grin in the rearview mirror. When our favorite part arrived, we leaned in together—our voices rising in playful unison, carrying that harmony into the open road.

It wasn't just singing. It was communion. Joy, ordinary and unguarded.

Even now, when I hear that song, it isn't the radio I think of— it's that drive. His voice behind me, mine overlapping his, both of us carried forward by the music.

I didn't know it then, but that ride would be our last trip together. That's still the image I hold—not the phone call that split the day in two.

The Hidden Moment

Sometime after midnight, I crept into the living room and

pulled one of his sports jerseys from the back of the closet.

It smelled like smoke and faint detergent, the particular blend that meant home to my child self. The fabric was softer than I remembered, worn thin in places, the stitched numbers rough beneath my fingers.

I curled into it on the couch and cried the kind of quiet cry you do when you don't want to wake anyone—shoulders shaking, breath held, tears soaking into the cloth.

No one saw that moment. No one needed to.

It was the first time I understood that grief has its own room inside you, a door you learn to open when the house goes still.

In the morning, I lifted the jersey back onto its hanger and slid it into the closet, as if returning it would restore some order.

The ache didn't stay behind with it.

It simply found its own place inside me.

The Physics of Grief

Later, I found language for what I was living.

> *"Grief is a series of adaptive tasks."*
> — Dr. William Worden

When loss reoccurs—especially another central figure—those tasks are compounded. It isn't starting over; it's swimming with weights you already know are too heavy.

> *"Grief isn't linear. It loops, doubles back, folds in on itself. Each new loss reawakens the pain of earlier ones."*
> — Elisabeth Kübler-Ross

That's why the second shockwave doesn't just feel familiar—It feels heavier.

Practical Anchors for the First Wave

⇒ **Assign a Point Person** – Let one trusted person handle updates so you're not reliving the shock with every call. After losing my stepfather, I asked one of my sisters to tell the others. That choice gave me a moment to breathe.

⇒ **Ground Yourself in the Smallest Tasks** – Pour a glass of water. Put both feet on the floor. Name three things you can see and touch.

⇒ **Accept Help You Didn't Plan For** – When someone offers to drive, cook, or make a call, say yes.

⇒ **Let Silence Be Your Shield** – You don't have to pick up every call or text. Silence isn't selfish—it's space to breathe.

⇒ **Do / Delegate / Drop** – Make a three-column list. Keep only what truly needs you. Ask one person to own the delegate column for a week.

Reflection: Surviving the First Wave

These aren't puzzles to solve—they're gentle invitations. Each question opens a space for your grief to speak, in a season when so much feels fragile and uncertain.

Take a slow breath. Let your shoulders soften. When you're ready, allow these questions to meet you where you are:

- Which responsibility am I carrying that doesn't truly belong to me?

- What is one small task I could release—even if it feels uncomfortable—to make space for my own healing?

- When have I worn the mask of "the strong one" while secretly breaking inside?

- If my grief had a sound—would it be silence, a sob, a scream, or something softer?

- What single, concrete act of care would help me breathe today?

- If I could tell *one safe person* the unedited truth, what would I say?

Your answers may shift as the days unfold. That's not a failure—it's part of the journey. May these questions give your grief room to breathe, and your heart room to rest.

Closing Thought

Grief folds you into new shapes. It teaches the weight of love and the fragility of life.

In those first moments, you may feel hollow. Lost. Like a part of you left with them.

But you are still here. Still breathing. And that, in itself, is strength.

This journey isn't about holding everything together perfectly. It's about being brave enough to rise, slowly and gently, carrying your love forward even when the ground feels unsteady.

The wave will crash. The weight will press. But you are not here to break. You are here to rise—slowly, gently, fiercely if you must.

One breath. One boundary. One step at a time.

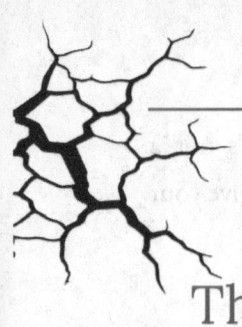

Chapter 2
The Undertow of Always Doing

"The early days after loss are heavy. Not just with what's been taken, but with what's suddenly placed in your hands."

I thought keeping busy would keep me afloat. But I learned that disappearing into doing only delayed the grief that needed to be felt.

Grief doesn't always arrive with tears. Sometimes it shows up as a to-do list.

You make the calls. Draft the program no one ever wants to write. Sit at the table with contracts and paperwork, reading line after line that feels less like documents and more like erasures.

They mean well—most of them do. But meaning well and doing well are not always the same.

Everyone thanks you for "being so strong." But underneath, you're not strong—you're just busy.

It looks like strength. It's really survival. And survival has its

20

own undertow—silent, relentless, pulling you farther from yourself before you even realize you're adrift.

Disappearing Into Doing

When my stepfather passed, I flew into town to be with my mom. Family filled the house in those first days—my aunts, uncles, cousins. They came with food, prayers, and stories meant to soothe. Her sister stayed close, a steady buoy in the storm.

I slipped quietly into logistics mode. I coordinated calls. Read through paperwork and contracts. Helped plan the funeral. Created structure.

It felt natural—necessary, even. She's been through enough, I told myself. I'll take this off her plate.

But I didn't realize how invisible my own grief had become—not just to others, but to myself.

I'd pass by the living room and hear bursts of laughter through tears as my family swapped stories—memories that lightened the heaviness for a moment.

While they grieved together, I was in the back room with papers spread across the table, juggling flower orders and funeral programs.

I wasn't in the room of grief.

I was in the room of tasks.

I was the silent engine keeping the ship moving through rough waters. But somewhere in that constant motion, I stopped noticing how cold and tired I was.

The undertow had already caught me—I just didn't realize how far it was pulling me from shore.

The Fixer's Roots

That undertow wasn't new. It had been tugging at me since childhood, shaping how I learned to cope with loss long before I had language for it.

I was eleven when my first stepfather passed—the man who filled our kitchen with riddles, who drove us to Burger King after school, who made flea market Saturdays feel like treasure hunts. His absence cracked our family open in ways I couldn't fully understand at the time.

In those first days, relatives swirled around my mother, checking on her, comforting her, carrying her through. But no one really paused to ask how we, the children, were doing. Our job was simple: behave. Be strong. Don't add to her burden.

So I did what I thought strength meant.

I made sandwiches. Fried eggs that turned out too hard. Cleaned dishes. Tried to keep my siblings and cousins in line. The smell of burned yolks filled the kitchen, but no one corrected me. In my mind, helping mattered more than getting it right.

No one asked how I was holding up. And in that environment, the thought never even occurred to me to ask myself.

The question *How are you doing?* wasn't part of my grief vocabulary. I was conditioned to give, not to receive.

So, when grief returned decades later, I slipped right back into that eleven-year-old's role—checking on Mom, checking on siblings, carrying my niece when needed, becoming the problem-solver instead of the one being asked about.

It felt familiar. Too familiar. The undertow had found me again, pulling me into old patterns before I even noticed.

The difference now was that I had my fem-pire of sister-friends, my cousins, my chosen circle. They were the ones who asked late at night:

"Hey. How are you, really?"

And that reminder—that my feelings mattered too—was what kept me from disappearing entirely.

Holding Compassion and Boundaries

This grief taught me something new: it wasn't only about caring for my parent. It was about not losing myself.

One night, just as I was laying my head down, my mother called asking me to come over. My old reflex would have been to get up immediately exhausted or not.

But I had already learned I couldn't pour from an empty cup. So, I tried something different:

> *"Mom, I'll come first thing in the morning, let's rest tonight."*
> Or: *"Once I wrap up this project, I'll come over and we'll take care of it together."*

At first, it felt uncomfortable—like I was letting her down.

I lay awake afterward, guilt buzzing in my chest.

But with practice, we developed a rhythm. She began to sense when I was working and gave me space. Yet there were still moments when she called, and I answered—because she's my mother, and that bond matters too.

It wasn't about choosing her or choosing myself. It was about learning the balance of both.

Therapist **Nedra Glover Tawwab** reminds us:

> "Boundaries are not just about saying
> no—they're about teaching others how to
> love us without losing ourselves."

And **Brené Brown** puts it bluntly:

> "Daring to set boundaries is about having
> the courage to love ourselves, even when we
> risk disappointing others."

Boundaries aren't rejection. They're invitations—to love with clarity, to give without depletion, and to honor both your parent's story and your own.

The Moment I Let Myself Receive

After one particularly long day of errands, calls, and caretaking, I collapsed on the couch with the lights still on. My phone buzzed. It was one of my fem-pire sisters.

> Checking in. Don't tell me
> you're fine … how are you,
> really?

Something cracked.

I started typing the usual I'm good, just tired—then erased it.

Instead, I wrote:

> I'm not okay. I feel like
> I'm holding everyone else's
> pieces and mine keep slipping.

The response came back instantly:

> Put one piece down. We'll
> hold it with you. You don't have
> to do this alone.

Tears blurred the screen. The living room was dark, cluttered with papers and mugs, but in that moment, I felt seen—not as the fixer, not as the strong one, but as a grieving daughter.

It reminded me that love isn't only in what we give—it's also in what we allow ourselves to receive.

Late-Night Truths

Later that week, when the house grew still, I truly heard the question I had been avoiding all day.

"How are you, really?"

And I paused. Because the truth? I didn't know. I hadn't stopped long enough to check in with myself. I was too busy holding space for everyone else.

But grief doesn't disappear just because you're busy. It waits. Quietly. Patiently. Until you're ready to feel it.

And when you do? It rushes in like a flood.

One evening, I found myself at the kitchen sink after everyone had gone to bed. A soft song came on the radio.

Without warning, tears began to fall.

I gripped the sponge like an anchor, dishwater running over my hands, stunned by how quickly the sadness surfaced.

No warning.
No build-up.
Just grief, raw and real, bubbling up in the stillness.

It was like surfacing from underwater—the undertow loosening its grip just long enough for me to gasp for air.

Expert Insight

Dr. Pauline Boss calls this *ambiguous loss*—when what's missing is not just the person, but the familiar patterns, rhythms, and roles you once relied on.

Brené Brown describes over-functioning as "a shield against vulnerability." It looks like love, but it's often fear—fear of what will happen if we stop, if we let grief close the distance.

And grief scholars **Margaret Stroebe** and **Henk Schut** remind us through their *Dual Process Model*: healthy grieving requires oscillating between loss-oriented tasks (feeling, remembering, honoring) and restoration-oriented tasks (managing daily life, finding new rhythms).

Living in only one mode, always doing or always drowning, prevents healing. It's the movement between the two that steadies us.

Practical Anchors for the Undertow

When you find yourself disappearing into "doing," try:

⇒ **Share the Updates Load** – Instead of fielding every "How's your mom, or dad?" call, set up a group text or rotate check-ins with siblings or cousins. Even that small handoff lightens the undertow.

⇒ **Block Grief Breaks** – Step away, even briefly. Sit in silence, sip tea, or walk outside—remind your body it still deserves rest.

⇒ **Let Them Reclaim Tasks** – Invite your parent back into small responsibilities when they're ready. Even folding laundry or paying a bill restores dignity.

⇒ **Ask for Specific Help** – Replace vague offers like *"Let me know if you need anything"* with one concrete ask: *"Could you bring dinner Wednesday night?"* Clear asks, create clear support.

⇒ **Track Your Emotional Temperature** – End each day with a pause: Did I feel my own grief today? If the answer is "no" for too many days, it's time to slow down and listen inward.

These anchors won't stop the undertow. But they will steady you enough to remember: you don't have to vanish to keep others afloat.

Reflection: Honoring Both Griefs

These aren't answers you must chase—they're gentle invitations. Each question gives you a way to sit with what changed the moment the news came, and how you are still carrying it now.

Take a slow breath. Let your body settle. When you're ready, allow these questions to meet you where you are:

- Where was I when the news came, and how has that place changed for me since?

- What is one detail from that day that still lingers most vividly in my mind?

- In what ways did time feel like it fractured—before and after?

29

- If I could name the emotion beneath the shock, what would it be?

- How did I step into action, and what did that reveal about me?

Your answers may soften or sharpen over time. That shifting is part of grief's rhythm. May these questions hold you steady as you breathe through the memory.

Closing Thought

Busyness may shield you for a time, but it cannot carry you forever. Tasks end. Papers get filed. Lists get crossed off. And when the silence returns, grief is still there, waiting to be felt.

You don't have to disappear in your parent's grief—or in your own tasks—to prove your love. Your healing matters too.

This isn't selfishness—it's survival. One pause. One boundary. One honest answer to the question: *How am I holding up today?*

Because strength isn't in doing everything. It's in daring to take the mask off and letting yourself be seen—messy, human, grieving, and still worthy of care.

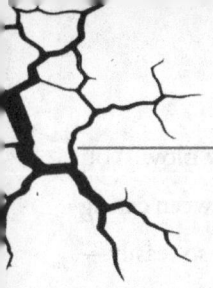

Chapter 3
When Holding on Holds You Back

"Sometimes the best way to help is to step aside and let them try." – Unknown

A t first, I believed helping meant doing everything. But I discovered that stepping back can be as loving as stepping in.

In the first months after my stepfather's passing, I moved through my mother's house like a quiet storm—opening drawers, fixing hinges, organizing papers, making sure everything ran smoothly.

If something was broken, I fixed it.
If something was scattered, I organized it.
I thought I was helping.

In truth, I was gripping so tightly to the role of helper that I was crowding out the small ways my mom could begin reclaiming her independence.

It wasn't intentional. It was instinct. When someone you love has been leveled by grief, you want to soften every blow. You want to take away every hard thing. But the line between caring for someone and taking over for them blurs so easily—especially when you don't pause to ask where that line should be.

One afternoon, I stood at the end of the driveway, staring at the long stretch of gravel my stepfather used to roll the trash can down. I thought: *That's too much for her now.*

Without asking, I called my sister.

> "We should find someone to come once a week and handle the trash for Mom," I said, already in problem-solving mode.

Later, I told my mom about the plan.
Her head tilted downward just slightly, her hands resting on the kitchen counter.

"I can do it," she said softly.

"No, Mom, you don't need to," I replied quickly. "We'll arrange for someone else."

She nodded, but it wasn't relief I saw in her eyes. It was something else.

Defeat.

It hit me—I hadn't even asked if she wanted help. I had decided for her. And in doing so, I had taken away one of the few everyday tasks she still had control over.

I stopped.

"You know what, Mom? I realize I may have overstepped. Do you want to keep doing it?"

She straightened a little.
"Yes. I can do it. I need to do it. I want to do it."

And she has. Every week since.

But I also told her, gently:
"Mom, if it ever gets too *heavy*—or if I'm not here and the others can't help—please let me know. We'll get someone to step in. You don't have to do it alone."

Her shoulders softened at that. It wasn't about taking the task away—it was about letting her know she had both freedom and backup.

Maybe you've been there too—so eager to ease the load that you accidentally stripped away someone's choice. If so, remember this: sometimes love isn't about doing more. It's about stepping back, so they can stand.

Family Dynamics in the Wake of Grief

After the trash can conversation, I began to see it more clearly: holding on too tightly doesn't always protect—it can suffocate. What I was learning with my mom, we as siblings also had to learn with each other. We weren't just juggling chores or schedules; we were wrestling with fear.

One evening, my siblings and I clashed about how much to step in—who could visit, who could take Mom places, who could be present when others lived out of town. Voices rose, tension sharp in the air. Each of us was tugging at the same rope in different ways, convinced our grip was the one holding everything together.

Then my brother cut through it:
"Why are we fighting about the details? This isn't about chores—it's about fear. We don't want to lose her too."

Silence. He was right.

After cooling down, we realized each of us was grieving in a different language. One equated independence with survival. Another equated help with love. I equated structure with safety. Beneath it all was the same ache: we were terrified of losing her twice—once to grief, and once to helplessness.

A few days later, I stood by the window and watched my

mother step out to the mailbox. That had always been my stepfather's task—the creak of the hinge, the shuffle of envelopes, the way he sorted them as he came back inside.

Now it was her.

She pulled out a thin stack of letters, bills placed on top, junk mail tucked beneath her arm. She carried them in with quiet steadiness.

It wasn't seamless. Letting go, and letting her find her rhythm, took time. Some weeks I still wanted to rush in, but she kept showing me—slowly, steadily—that she could do it.

What looked like routine was something deeper. It was resilience disguised as ritual. A small act that whispered: *I'm still here. I'm still capable. I'm still me—even if different than before.*

That's when my brother's words echoed back: this wasn't about chores. It was about agency—the fragile but vital ability to choose and act. Without it, grief deepens. With it, even small moments become stepping-stones toward healing.

I've since learned what psychologists like **Kenneth Doka** caution: when someone is constantly praised for being the "strong one," their own grief can be overlooked—and their parent's growth stunted. **Albert Bandura** calls agency not just the act of doing, but the belief that you *can*. And **Robert Neimeyer** puts it beautifully: healing comes not only from remembering who we've lost, but from reconstructing meaning in who we are becoming.

Watching my mom reclaim that belief—one small act at a time—reminded me that resilience doesn't arrive fully formed. It grows in the doing. Whether it's hauling a trash can, cooking a simple meal, or sorting the mail, these aren't chores. They're declarations:

I am still here. I am capable. I am becoming.

Reflection: Loosen Without Letting Go

These aren't puzzles to solve—they're invitations. Each question gives you space to notice the difference between helping that heals and helping that hinders.

Take a slow breath. Let your shoulders soften. When you're ready, allow these questions to meet you where you are:

- When have I stepped in for my parent without asking if they wanted help?

- What task or ritual might actually strengthen my parent's sense of independence if I let them keep it?

- What was I afraid would happen if I stepped back?

- How do my siblings or family members express their love through "help," and how is it different from mine?

- What would it look like to offer both freedom *and* backup—the reassurance that my parent is not alone, even when they choose to do something themselves?

Your answers may shift over time, just as roles shift. That's not failure—it's growth. May these questions remind you that stepping back can be as loving as stepping in.

Closing Thought

Grief asks a lot of us, but it never asked for perfection.

Sometimes, the most courageous thing you can do is release the rope—trusting that others can and will step in. Because the moment you loosen your grip, you create space for something surprising to happen:

They rise.
You breathe.
And the tide feels just a little less heavy.

Loosening my grip didn't mean walking away—it meant walking beside her differently. And as I began to see, grief wasn't only changing her routines. It was reshaping the woman I had always known.

Chapter 4
The Quiet Shift You Don't See Coming

"The death of a spouse doesn't just break your parent's heart—it reshapes their identity. And sometimes, that shift reshapes yours too."

I didn't expect that. I thought grief would change my mom, but I wasn't prepared for how quietly it would begin reshaping me.

When a parent's partner dies, everything shifts. The person you once turned to may suddenly feel fragile. Their sharpness softens. Their routines unravel. It's not just their partner who's missing—it's part of who they used to be.

You grieve the person they lost. But you also grieve the version of your parent you once knew. And when you try to hold too tightly to who they were—or who you were—you discover that holding on can hold you back.

This dual grief—yours and theirs—requires a new kind of relationship. One rooted not in who they were, but in who they are now becoming.

I saw this firsthand with my mom. In those first months, she repeated the same words almost daily:

"It's just so much. I don't even know where to begin."

Her voice carried the weight of someone staring at a thousand broken pieces, unable to see where the first fit belonged. She had always had her partner—her balance, her sounding board. Without him, even ordinary decisions looked like mountains.

I could feel her fear, the overwhelm of facing a thousand unknowns at once. And I had a choice: push her to move faster, or remind her gently—again and again—"Mom, it's one step at a time. Just one."

At first, I had to say it multiple times a day. The fog of grief is thick, and you don't always see your way out. But reminding her—and reminding myself—gave us something to hold onto: one step, not the whole staircase.

Maybe you've been there too—sitting across from someone you love, hearing their fear, feeling your own, and wondering if either of you will ever find the first step. If so, know this: you're not alone in the fog.

Even as I repeated those words to her, I hadn't yet realized how much this loss was reshaping her—and me. It took my sister's perspective to open my eyes to the deeper shift happening beneath the surface.

A Sibling's Lens

One evening, I was on the phone with my sister after another long day of tending to details. I confessed how drained I felt, caught between helping Mom and managing my own emotions.

She was quiet for a moment before saying, "You know, I see her differently now. She's not just our mother—she's a woman trying to figure out who she is without him. It's like watching someone rebuild themselves from the inside out."

Her words stopped me. I had been so focused on holding tasks together that I hadn't paused to see the deeper shift. To her, it wasn't just about grief—it was about identity.

That perspective helped me soften, not just toward Mom, but toward myself. We weren't only managing logistics. We were witnessing transformation.

Patience Over Ridicule

I first saw this lesson years earlier, with my grandmother. As she aged, her memory began to slip, and her temper sometimes followed. I was old enough to notice but not wise enough to respond well. My sharp corrections, "I just said that" landed harder than I realized.

The lesson returned years later like a mirror when I caught myself rushing my mother through her own grief. I heard the edge in my voice, saw the disappointment in her posture—shoulders slumping just slightly—and realized I was wounding where I meant to help.

In my quiet time, my spirit nudged me: *Lead with love. If she asked three times, answer three times—with patience, not judgment.*

That shift changed everything. What once bred tension began to build tenderness. Grace, I realized, doesn't erase the frustration. It transforms it into something that sustains both of us.

Patience didn't just change my responses—it also changed how I understood stillness. What once looked like stagnation began to feel like part of the process.

The Stillness Before the Doing

One of the hardest lessons was learning that stillness has a place in grief.

There were days when nothing seemed to happen—clothes still hanging in the closet, papers untouched on the table, her frame quiet in the chair by the window. At first, I worried these pauses meant we were stuck, sliding backward instead of forward.

But over time, I saw the truth: processing often comes before doing. The silence wasn't failure—it was her way of gathering enough strength to move again.

Grief isn't always visible in action. Sometimes it's buried in the moments that look like nothing at all. Allowing her those pauses—and allowing myself to sit with them—became part of how we both kept going.

It's like soil resting in winter before the spring. What looks barren is actually preparing for growth.

Maybe you've seen that too—what looks like "nothing happening" is often the quiet work of grief, slowly preparing for the next small step forward.

Practical Anchors for Navigating the Quiet Shift

Grief doesn't just show up in tears or memories. It shows up in the laundry basket, the bills, the dishes, the mail. Ordinary tasks carry extraordinary weight because they whisper: *life is still moving, even here.*

Instead of rushing through these moments, I learned to see them as anchors—small ways for my mother to reclaim her rhythm, and small ways for me to honor her process.

⇒ **Name the Change Without Blame.**
A gentle, "I've noticed you've been quieter lately— how are you feeling?" created room for honesty without shame.

⇒ **Preserve Small Rituals.**
Even scaled-back traditions carried power. Brewing coffee and sitting with her for ten quiet minutes each morning became our new anchor.

⇒ **Balance the Roles.**
Writing down what she once managed and what I now carried helped me see where I could hand back small responsibilities when she was ready.

⇒ **Honor the Pause.**
Long silences didn't mean failure. They meant processing.

⇒ **Invite Their Wisdom Back In.**
Even fragile, our parents still hold lifetimes of insight. Asking for her advice—on a recipe, a memory, even a family story—restored dignity and reminded her she was more than her grief.

These weren't big breakthroughs. They were ordinary moments with extraordinary weight—the kind that stitched us back together slowly.

Reflection: Noticing Your Needs

When I paused to look inward, I realized the shift wasn't only hers—it was mine too. You may find the same.

- How has my parent shifted since the loss—and how have I?

- What part of them am I holding onto that may never fully return?

- Where can I steady with firmer boundaries—or soften with deeper compassion—so we both keep balance?

- What rituals, no matter how small, still tether us to connection?

These aren't demands for answers. *They're gentle mirrors.* Each question opens a space to see both your parent and yourself more clearly—as you are now, not as you once were.

Closing Thought

Grief reshapes two lives at once.

Your parent may never return to who they were before, and you may never return to who you were before. But that doesn't mean love has disappeared. It means both of you are slowly learning how to meet each other again—awkwardly, tenderly, in this new terrain.

Patience becomes the bridge. Every small ritual kept, every pause honored, every moment you choose compassion over correction creates space for transformation—space for your parent to rebuild and for you to breathe.

The quiet shift isn't about replacing what was lost. It's about discovering who you both are now—and how love still lives here. One step. One pause. One fragile, surprising laugh at a time.

Chapter 5
When Joy Feels Like Betrayal

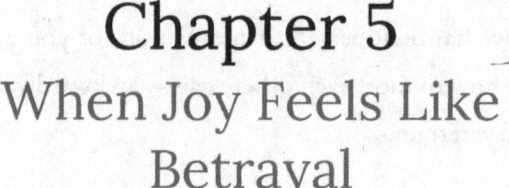

"When someone you love dies, it feels wrong to keep living. But healing doesn't dishonor them—it honors you both."

F or a long time, I mistook joy for disloyalty. But I learned that laughter doesn't erase love—it carries it forward.

There comes a moment after loss—after the funeral, after the calls slow down—when you think: Maybe I should do something normal.

Maybe it's brunch with a friend. Picking up the knitting needles again. Returning to a hobby you once loved. Or laughing at a meme that lands just right.

And then it hits: the guilt.

The Laugh That Surprised Me

The first time I went to brunch after my stepfather passed, I kept looking around wondering if people could tell. Sunlight streamed through the café windows, warming the tops of glass syrup bottles. Cinnamon waffles and espresso mingled in the air.

I smiled when the waiter poured coffee. I even joked with the friend across from me.

But inside, it felt like I was borrowing someone else's life. The world around me was bright, loud, and fast—and I felt slow, muted, almost invisible.

Still, I showed up. And for that moment, showing up was enough.

The Slow Creep of Guilt

It sneaks in quietly. Not because you did anything wrong, but because it feels too soon to feel okay. Too soon to enjoy anything. Too soon to let life in.

Grief researcher **Dr. Alan Wolfelt** calls this mourner's guilt—the uneasy sense that joy is somehow a betrayal.

But he reminds us:

> "The capacity to feel joy while grieving is not a
> sign of disrespect. It's a sign of resilience."

His words stayed with me, but they didn't sink in right away. It wasn't until later, when joy slipped out of me unexpectedly, that I began to understand what he meant.

The First Laugh

I remember the first time I laughed after my stepfather passed. Really laughed. I can't recall the exact joke—something my niece said about Grandpa probably playing cards with angels and winning.

The laugh startled me. It felt foreign in my own throat. I worried someone might hear and think I was "over it." But no one did. The judgment was mine alone. That laugh was a release. A reminder that I was still here. And deep down, I believe he would've wanted that.

As I sat with the sound of it, something shifted. Laughter, I realized, wasn't replacing grief, it was remembering differently. Each laugh carried a thread of him: his humor, his easy wit, his way of lightening even the heaviest room. My laughter didn't erase him. It echoed him. And in that echo, I found a new kind of closeness I hadn't expected.

That moment taught me something I hadn't yet admitted: the return of joy wasn't the enemy.

The real struggle was the guilt that followed.

Why Joy Feels Dangerous

Joy changes the room. It interrupts the quiet ache you've gotten used to carrying. And that disruption can feel disloyal.

Part of this is cultural. Many societies expect grief to be solemn, measured, restrained. But others do it differently. In Mexican tradition, Día de los Muertos is a festival of color, music, and food—welcoming spirits back with celebration. In parts of Ghana, funerals are vibrant, with drumming and dancing to honor the life lived.

These traditions remind us that joy and grief are not enemies, they're companions.

I carried that truth quietly, unsure if I believed it for myself—until one ordinary afternoon, music put it to the test.

When Music Sneaks In

One afternoon, driving my mom to the grocery store, *Bohemian Rhapsody* came on the radio. Without thinking, I started singing—quietly at first, then louder as Freddie Mercury's voice filled the car.

My mom glanced over, and to my surprise, she joined in. Her voice cracked, but she smiled, tapping her fingers lightly against the seat.

51

And then, as the song swelled, certain lines landed differently than they ever had before. They carried weight I hadn't noticed before his passing—words that, in that moment, felt like him speaking directly to me: *Keep going. Carry on. Even now.*

It caught me off guard. I had always loved the song, but grief tuned my ears to a new frequency. What once was just music became a message, a bridge.

For a few minutes, grief loosened its grip. The car was full of something bigger—music, memory, and life itself spilling over. By the time we pulled into the parking lot, we were laughing, catching our breath between verses.

Joy had snuck in, uninvited but welcome. And instead of feeling like betrayal, it felt like permission.

Grief and Joy Can Coexist

Which is why guilt doesn't have to be the final word. Grief and joy can sit at the same table. Some days grief takes the head seat. Other days, joy passes the bread. But both belong.

You don't have to choose between honoring your loved one and honoring your own life. Both can be true.

Psychologist George Bonanno, a pioneer in resilience research, found that most people demonstrate an unexpected capacity for recovery after loss. He notes:

> "The ability to rebound remains the norm throughout adult life."

Practical Anchors: Inviting Joy Back In

Inviting joy back isn't about pretending you're fine. It's about letting life trickle in at a pace your heart can hold.

⇒ **Start Small** – A walk in the park. A favorite meal. Something low-stakes that feels doable.

⇒ **Blend Joy with Memory** – Order their favorite dessert. Play their favorite '70s track while cooking. Let their presence be part of the moment.

⇒ **Set a Gentle Boundary** – If it feels overwhelming, give the activity a time frame. "I'll stay for an hour" can take the pressure off.

⇒ **Name the Guilt** – If it surfaces, ask: Is this guilt mine, or is it tied to what I think others expect of me?

⇒ **Reflect Afterwards** – Journal or voice-note the emotions that came up. No judgment, just witness.

⇒ **Share Joy Out Loud** – Tell someone close, "I laughed today—and it felt strange." Naming it helps normalize it.

Reflection: Guilt and Grace

Exhale slowly. Notice where joy feels heavy in your body, like a stone you're not sure you should lift.

- What ordinary joy have I felt guilty for reaching toward?

- Where could I welcome grace back in—without apology, without shame?

- How might I carry their memory into joy, like a current moving alongside me rather than against me?

- Who in my circle could remind me that joy is not disloyalty but resilience?

- What small joy feels safe enough to practice this week?

These aren't permission slips. They are reminders that joy and grief can coexist—and your willingness to hold both is its own form of grace.

Closing Thought

Grief is a long road. But joy is not betrayal—it's survival. Let yourself return to life gently.

You're not leaving them behind. You're learning how to carry them forward.

Each laugh. Each breath. Each small joy is not a betrayal—it's proof you're still carrying them with you.

And yet, as you let life back in, another truth emerges: not every gesture of comfort comforts. Some words meant to encourage land like dismissal. Some offers of help press heavier than the grief itself.

Learning to navigate those moments is part of the work too.

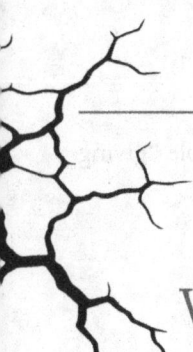

Chapter 6
When the Help Isn't Helping

"Support is only helpful when it honors your reality—not when it adds to your burden."

By the time I began letting joy back in, I also discovered another truth: not every gesture of comfort feels like comfort. Some support heals, but some quietly harms.

I thought help would always feel like comfort. But grief taught me otherwise: not all help actually helps. Some support sustains, and some silently drains.

In the weeks following a loss, people show up. They show up with food, with advice, with scriptures and stories, with pies wrapped in foil and quotes taped to index cards.

The Unhelpful Help

Sometimes the "help" arrives in the form of control: Someone takes over decisions you didn't ask them to make, rearranging your plans without consulting you.

Other times, it's silence disguised as respect—people "giving you space" but offering no tangible support.

And then there are the comments that sting:

> "At least they're in a better place."
> "God doesn't give us more than we can handle."
> "You're so strong."

You smile. Nod. Say thank you. But inside, you're crumbling.

Strength wasn't the goal. Survival was. And platitudes don't patch grief. They just push it deeper underground.

The Day I Shut the Door

I remember the day I politely shut the door on someone's kindness.

Not because I was angry—because I was exhausted.

They had come by unannounced, holding a warm casserole and a stack of old photographs. *Thought you'd like to remember the good times,* they said, stepping inside without waiting for me to answer.

I smiled, because that's what you're taught to do when someone means well. But I didn't have the energy to hold space for their memories or absorb their version of comfort, which, in that moment, cost me more than it gave.

So I thanked them, hugged them, and gently shut the door.

Then I sat on the couch and cried—not because of what they did, but because I finally recognized what I needed...and I didn't yet know how to ask for it.

That moment showed me how blurry the line can be between help that heals and help that harms. And it wasn't the only time.

The Road Trip Breakdown

A few weeks later, my mom and I took a short road trip to visit family. It was our first time back in the city where my stepfather had passed away. The air felt heavy even before we arrived.

Halfway through the visit, our car broke down. We ended up staying with relatives while we figured out how to get it repaired.

My mom immediately blamed herself.
"Your father would've checked the oil. He would've made sure the car was ready."
Her voice cracked under the weight of regret.

As we tried to sort out next steps, one of my aunts shook her head and said, almost casually:
"Wow. The vehicle has died like your father. It's like everything is dying."

My mom and I froze. We looked at each other, startled.

I took a breath and said firmly: *"No.* He has passed, but not everything dies with him. This car will run again. And so will we."

Her words had landed like a stone, but I chose not to carry it.

Eventually, the car was repaired and back on the road—a quiet reminder that not everything broken stays broken. Life, too, finds ways to move forward.

That moment stayed with me, not just because of the inconvenience, but because of how quickly someone's attempt to name the grief almost buried us in it. It taught me that not all words bring comfort, and sometimes the most healing response is choosing which words not to take in.

Holding My Parent While Holding Myself

Back home, the same pattern kept showing up. There were days I'd sit beside my mom, filling the silences with quiet reassurance, making choices she didn't have the energy to face.

And then, just as I'd exhale, the phone would ring. Someone needed an update. Someone else suggested I cheer her up with a night out—as if a quick return to old routines could shortcut the grief.

But she wasn't ready. She needed time to simply be.

By the time I hung up, the moment I had been holding for myself was gone. I hadn't had space to cry. Or sit still. Or feel the absence.

Everyone meant well, but no one realized how thinly stretched I was—trying to carry her through while quietly unraveling inside.

It took me longer than I wanted to admit, and more guilt than I expected, to finally realize: I could say no.

Not just for her sake—
but for mine.

Permission to Set Boundaries

These moments, at the door, on the road, on the phone—taught me the same lesson:

You can be grateful and still exhausted.
You can appreciate someone's effort and still say, *"This isn't what I need right now."*

Support that costs more than it gives is not support—it's noise.

You are allowed to name what helps and what hurts.

You are allowed to say:

⇒ "Thank you, but I'm not up for visitors today."

⇒ "I appreciate the thought, but I need quiet."

⇒ "I know you mean well, but that comment didn't land well with me."

Grief already asks so much of you. Don't let someone else's version of "help" ask for more.

Practical Scripts: Responding with Honesty and Grace

Sometimes it helps to have the words ready. Here are a few ways to respond when "help" misses the mark:

To a platitude:

> Them: "At least they're in a better place."
> You: "I know you want to comfort me, and I appreciate that. What helps me most right now is simply having someone listen."

To an unasked-for task:

> Them: "I already rearranged everything, so you don't

have to think about it."

You: "I'm grateful for the effort, but I'd like to be part of those decisions. Could you check with me first?"

To a visit you can't manage:

Them: "I'll swing by later this afternoon."

You: Thank you but today isn't a good day. Could we set up another time?"

These aren't rejections. They're gentle boundary lines that protect your healing.

Redefining Help in Real Life

From pies at the door to phone calls that drained me, I learned this: the best help is the kind that lightens more than it weighs.

Sometimes, the best help looks like:

- A quiet ride to the grocery store.
- A text that says, "No need to reply—just checking in."
- A meal left on the porch with no knock.
- Someone simply sitting beside you, saying nothing.

Megan Devine, author of It's OK That You're Not OK, captures it perfectly:
"Some things cannot be fixed. They can only be carried."

True help doesn't try to fix your grief. It simply helps you carry it.

Cultural & Generational Layers

Of course, what feels like help often depends on context.

In some cultures, showing up unannounced with food is a deep act of love. In others, it's seen as intrusive.

Older generations may believe that doing something, anything—is better than doing nothing. Younger ones may lean toward emotional space and asking permission before showing up.

Recognizing these differences can help you respond with grace. But it doesn't mean you have to accept help in a way that costs you more than it gives.

As grief counselor Dr. Alan Wolfelt reminds us:

> *"What mourners need most is not advice, but presence. Not fixing, but witnessing."*

5 Questions to Ask Before Accepting Help

⇒ Does this offer meet a real need I have right now?

⇒ Will accepting this drain or replenish me?

⇒ Do I have the emotional capacity to engage with the giver?

⇒ Could I modify their offer so it works better for me?

⇒ Am I saying yes out of gratitude—or out of guilt?

Reflection: Help that Heals

Pause. Picture the last time someone offered help. Feel into your body: did it lighten you, or weigh you down?

- What kind of support feels like a lifeline—and what drags me under?

- Where have I accepted "help" that left me emptier instead of steadier?

- What support do I long for but haven't found the courage to ask for?

- Where have I confused gratitude with obligation?

- How can I name the help that steadies me, like an oar keeping me in rhythm with the waves?

These aren't demands to make—they're clarities to claim. Knowing what helps and what hurts is the first step toward asking for the support you truly need.

Closing Thought

From pies at the door, to words that stung on the road, to calls that left me weary, I learned this: not all help helps.

And naming that doesn't make you ungrateful—it makes you honest.

You deserve support that sustains you, not drains you. Support that meets you where you are, not where someone else thinks you should be.

One boundary. One breath. One true connection at a time.

Part II

Illustration by Mischere V. Kyles

The Shifts & The Shadows

G rief doesn't disappear. It reshapes.

Your parent may look familiar but feel altered—quieter, more fragile, or suddenly sharp in ways you don't recognize. You may find yourself unsettled by small changes: the tone of their voice, your own unexpected laughter, the silence that lingers longer than before.

These are the shadows—subtle, often invisible at first. Unlike the first wave of loss, they don't crash loudly. They seep in, shifting the ground beneath you until nothing feels quite the same.

Part Two is about learning to walk in those shadows without losing your footing. To honor your parent's changes without erasing your own. To protect love with boundaries that steady rather than smother. To recognize that healing isn't about erasing pain—it's about finding a rhythm where sorrow and life move together.

This is the quiet, complicated terrain of the long middle: where survival deepens into something steadier, and where you begin to rebuild trust in a world forever changed.

The shadows will come. But they don't have to steal your light.

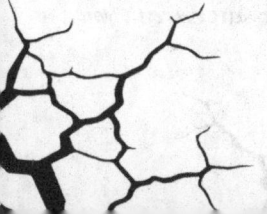

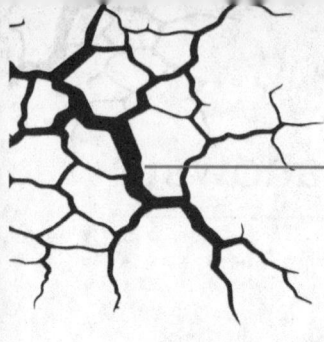

Chapter 7
Time Doesn't Heal the Way You Think

"Grief doesn't work on a schedule. It works on a heartbeat."

I thought time would close the wound. But time only changed the shape of it—and taught me that healing is not forgetting.

Grief casts shadows. Some come from memory. Others from expectation. And one of the heaviest shadows is time itself—the belief that healing has an expiration date, that after enough months pass you should be "better," "stronger," "back to normal."

There's a moment in every grief journey when someone, well-meaning or not—asks questions like:

> "How's your mom doing now?"
> "Are things getting back to normal yet?"
> "You seem better—are you feeling like yourself again?"

And behind each question lingers a subtle pressure: *Aren't you done yet?*

Maybe you've felt it too—the way people measure your grief against months on a calendar, as if healing had a stopwatch. But grief isn't a project. It's not something you complete and check off a list. It's a recalibration of everything you thought you knew about life, love, and yourself.

The Pressure to Move On

We live in a world that celebrates the bounce back: the quick return to work, the smile at social gatherings, the appearance of "moving on."

But what if the bounce back isn't real? What if it's a mask? What if the grief is still there—just hidden beneath politeness and productivity?

When you're supporting a grieving parent, the pressure compounds. You may feel obligated to be "strong" for them, to hold back your emotions so theirs can have room. But over time, the mask gets heavy. And no one sees how long you've been carrying it.

The Smile That Was Misunderstood

About four months after my stepfather died, one of my cousins came to visit my mother. We were standing in the kitchen when they said, almost casually:

"Oh, you look good and you're smiling—you must be getting over things."

My mom paused. Then she replied firmly:

"Getting over? No. Smiling doesn't mean I'm getting over. He'll always be a part of my life."

Her response rang like a bell. To an outsider, her smile looked like progress. But I had seen the nights of silence. The way she drifted toward his desk in the TV room—his desk, always cluttered with crossword puzzles and loose pens. After he passed, she sometimes sat there quietly, just resting her hand on the worn edge, as if reaching for him in the simplest way she could.

Time was moving forward, yes. But it wasn't erasing—it was reshaping. Life wasn't "back to normal." It was slowly becoming something entirely new.

As grief expert **Dr. William Worden** reminds us:

> *"Time alone does not heal grief. It is what we do with that time that matters."*

Even the Experts Get It Wrong

A close friend of mine lost her mother a few years ago. Even now, Mother's Day is almost unbearable.

She once told me about a doctor's appointment where, in casual conversation, he asked:

"You're not over it yet?"

That one sentence cut deeper than she expected. She walked out not just with a prescription, but with the reminder that even professionals can treat grief like a problem to be solved instead of a love that still needs space.

If even doctors can impose timelines, it's no wonder family and friends do too.

The Game She Couldn't Play Yet

For years, my mom and stepdad bowled together in a local league. It wasn't just a game—it was their rhythm, their laughter, their community.

After he died, invitations came. Friends encouraged her: "Come back, keep busy, it will help."

But bowling without him wasn't just bowling. It was an empty lane, an empty chair, a glaring reminder of his absence.

It took months before she could even consider stepping foot in the alley again. And when she did, it wasn't triumphant. It was cautious, tender—like walking onto sacred ground.

That moment taught me something: moving forward doesn't mean rushing back to what you loved. Sometimes it means giving grief enough time to soften so those places stop hurting quite as much.

Grief Comes in Waves, Not Milestones

Some days, you feel lighter. Then something small—an old voicemail, a song drifting from a store speaker, the smell of hickory smoke from a neighbor's grill—pulls you under again.

For me, it happened when I heard a tune my stepdad used to hum. I froze mid-aisle, tears blurring my vision. Grief had no interest in the calendar. It moved like a tide, coming and going on its own rhythm.

That doesn't mean you've failed. It means you're human.

Grief is not a straight line. It's a tide. And healing doesn't mean closure—it means learning to float. Floating doesn't always look graceful. Sometimes it's sobbing in the car before a meeting. Sometimes it's laughter at a memory followed by tears five minutes later.

Floating is not about strength. It's about letting go enough to be held—because fighting the water only pulls you under.

Letting Go of Other People's Timelines

You are not behind. You are not doing it wrong. You are not obligated to grieve quickly so others feel more comfortable.

Once, pressured by others, my mom agreed to attend a gathering just weeks after my stepfather's passing. People meant well, hoping it would "lift her spirits." Instead, it left her hollow—reminded more of what was missing than what was present.

The lesson was clear: moving forward isn't about speed. It's about readiness.

So let go of the inner voice that whispers:

- *"It's been six months—shouldn't I be over this?"*

- *"My siblings have moved on—why can't I?"*

- *"I need to be strong for my parent."*

Grief doesn't expire. And you don't owe anyone your healing on demand.

Practical Anchors: Living Beyond the Calendar

⇒ **Notice Your Rhythm** – Pay attention to when the

waves hit. What stirs them? What soothes them?

⇒ **Challenge the Pressure** – If someone asks, "Aren't you better yet?" try: *"I'm moving at my own pace."*

⇒ **Ritualize Time** – Light a candle, cook their favorite meal, or mark anniversaries with intention. Rituals give grief a voice.

⇒ **Give Yourself Permission** – Cry again. Laugh again. Remember again. None of it means you're "doing it wrong."

Reflection: Time and Truth

Take a breath, release the clock. Grief isn't measured in minutes—it's felt in moments. Let these questions sit with you:

- Where have I felt pressured to "move on" before my heart was ready?
- What does healing mean for me—does it mean forgetting, or carrying differently?
- When has time felt like an ally, and when has it felt like a burden?
- How can I honor anniversaries, holidays, or ordinary days without forcing myself into a timeline that isn't mine?

These questions don't ask for deadlines—they ask for honesty. Your pace is sacred. Your rhythm matters.

Closing Thought

Time alone doesn't heal.

What heals is the love you carry forward, the space you give yourself to feel, and the grace you extend to your own slow becoming.

Healing isn't about forgetting—it's about remembering with less fear.

So if you're smiling today, let it be because you found a moment of light, not because you felt pressured to look "better."

Because true healing has never been about getting over. It's about learning to live within the rhythm of a changed life.

Not a deadline. A reshaping. Still whole. Still worthy. Still yours.

And just when you think you've found that rhythm, grief reminds you—it doesn't knock. It lets itself in. Uninvited, unannounced, slipping into the cracks of ordinary life.

That's where the next shadow begins.

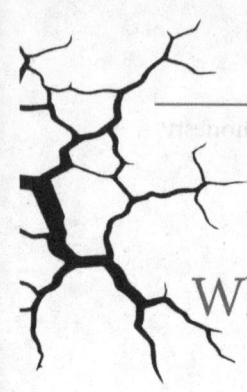

Chapter 8
When Grief Becomes the Uninvited Guest

"What is grief, if not love persevering?" —
WandaVision

I once assumed grief had an expiration date. But I learned it lingers—sometimes quietly, sometimes loudly—until it finds its place beside you.

Grief is not a guest you invite.

It barges in—through papers, objects, and moments you thought were safe. No warning. No knock. Just presence.

The Document That Undid Me

I was sitting at the table helping my mom sort estate documents for my stepfather when my hand froze.

I had expected forms, bank statements, maybe insurance policies.

What I didn't expect was to come across my first stepfather's death certificate.

I had never seen it before. And the sight of it broke me.

In an instant, I wasn't an adult balancing paperwork. I was a little girl again, standing in a hospital waiting room, clutching my siblings' hands as the world collapsed. Tears blurred the page.

And with it came the old fragments I thought I had tucked away—Burger King booths with fries and milkshakes, riddles tossed across the kitchen counter, Saturday mornings wandering flea markets where he taught me that beauty could be found in overlooked places.

That day took me off guard. I was still raw from losing my second stepfather, but holding that certificate revealed something deeper: I had been carrying an old wound I didn't know was still open. His loss had never fully left me. And in that moment, the ache of both losses lived side by side.

If you've ever been undone by something small—an unexpected document, a smell, a sound—you know how suddenly grief barges back in, reminding you it was never gone.

Not Over It

In the weeks following my stepfather's passing, my mother confessed one night through tears:

"I'm sorry. I'm just not there yet. I miss him. I'm

Not there yet"

Her words carried a weight only love can.

I reminded her softly:

"It's not about getting over, Mom. It's about
moving with."

Grief doesn't erase. It reshapes. It asks not for closure, but for companionship.

The Chair, the Hat, the Truck

Grief slipped into the smallest spaces of our house.

The porch, where his blue folding chair still sat. Weeks passed before my mother could even walk near it without pausing.

The cowboy hat by the entryway—creased from years of wear—remained like a silent sentinel.

Dust gathered in the brim, but his presence lingered all the same.

And then came the truck.

At first, my mother didn't want anyone to drive it. The scent of his cologne, the faint trace of cigarette smoke—it was too much. Too raw.

But my youngest sister eventually began to drive it. For her, sliding behind the wheel wasn't about moving on—it was about holding on. The smell, the worn steering wheel, the seat he once adjusted—all of it became her way of staying connected.

Maybe for you it isn't a truck. Maybe it's a sweater hanging in the closet, a playlist on the radio, or the empty side of the bed. For one person, it's unbearable. For another, it's a lifeline. Grief gives each of us a different language.

The Empty Grill

Grief doesn't just haunt objects. It shadows traditions too.

For my mom, the Fourth of July had always meant the grill— my stepfather rising early, seasoning ribs while hickory smoke curled into the summer air.

That first holiday after he died, the grill stayed cold. None of us could bear it. Instead, we went to a baseball game.

Hot dogs in hand, fireworks bursting overhead, we found a new way to sit together in our loss.

It wasn't the same. But it was survivable.

Sometimes grief forces you to rewrite traditions. Not because the old ones didn't matter—but because the love in them is too strong to ignore. Choosing something new isn't erasure. It's mercy.

Carried, Not Fixed

> Grief educator Megan Devine writes: *"Some things in life cannot be fixed. They can only be carried."*

Her words echo every object, every ritual, every avoided porch chair. Grief doesn't demand we get over. It asks us to carry—with tenderness, with patience, with room for both sorrow and light.

Practical Anchors: Moving With, Not Over

⇒ **Allow the Echoes** – Notice what feels impossible right now. You don't have to rush back. Avoidance is not weakness; it's care.

⇒ **Redefine Progress** – Smiling, laughing, or sharing a meal isn't betrayal. It's a reminder that humanity holds both ache and joy.

⇒ **Honor Their Space** – Sit at their desk, walk their favorite path, or play their music. Let these be bridges, not barriers.

⇒ **Gentle Scripts:**

   ○ For yourself: *"I can't face the porch today.*

That's okay."

- o For a parent: *"We don't have to light the grill this year. Let's choose something gentler."*

- o For siblings: *"If the truck brings you closer to him, keep driving it. That's your way of carrying."*

Reflection: Carrying Forward

Close your eyes. Picture the spaces they once filled—their chair, their laugh, their rituals. Then gently ask:

- Where have I pressured myself to "get over" instead of learning to carry?

- What everyday places or objects still echo with their presence?

- Which traditions feel too heavy to keep, and which ones could be tenderly rewritten?

- How might honoring their presence in the ordinary become a way of carrying them forward?

These aren't instructions for moving past. They're invitations to move with.

Closing Thought

Grief never knocks. It barges in—through documents, through chairs and hats, through trucks that smell of cologne, through holidays that no longer feel the same.

It doesn't ask you to forget. It asks you to carry—with pauses, with substitutions, with whispers of *"I'm not there yet."*

Grief doesn't end. It lingers, it reshapes, it reminds.

And it reshapes not just you, but the whole family—because the same loss is carried in different languages.

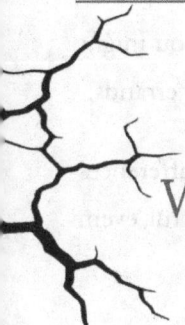

Chapter 9
When Family Grieves Differently

"Same loss, different language."

At first, I believed we would grieve the same way. But I learned that even in the same loss, we speak different languages of sorrow.

Grief doesn't show up the same way in every person, even when you've all lost the same person.

One cries at every memory. Another cracks jokes to break the tension. Someone else goes silent, keeping it all inside. Then there's the sibling who seems "unbothered," and the cousin who suddenly wants to take control of everything. Same loss. Different language.

The Grief Gap

This gap, the space between how you grieve and how others do, can feel like a second loss. You might want to talk about

85

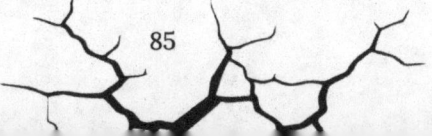

memories, while someone else avoids the subject. You might crave silence, while another fills the air with music or errands.

And when you're already raw with grief, those differences don't just feel awkward—they can feel personal. Hurtful, even.

When Roles Clash

After my stepfather's death, I was the one who stayed hands-on—navigating estate details, meeting with companies, making sure nothing slipped through the cracks.

Others showed up in their own ways. A sibling dropped off home-cooked meals. Another cleaned the shed when asked. One planned an outing to a play, giving my mother something to look forward to.

And my youngest sister—well, she began driving his blue truck. At first, it caused me concern. She often left town on business trips, and I caught myself questioning: Why isn't she around more? But over time I realized—I was only seeing absence, not her way of grieving. That truck, still carrying his cologne in the seat, became her refuge. Out on the highway, she found the space to carry her loss in motion.

Different from mine, yes, but still grief. Still love.

Maybe you've noticed the same tension in your own family—

wondering why someone else isn't showing up like you are, only to realize their grief is simply speaking in another voice.

And yes, there were moments it stung. I'd be knee-deep in paperwork while someone else dropped off dinner and left. More than once I caught myself thinking: Why am I carrying all of this while they get to do the lighter work?

But grief has a way of humbling your assumptions.

It took time, but I came to see that different didn't mean absent. Their support may not have looked like mine, but it still mattered. Once I stopped measuring their actions against my own, I could see the meaning in each contribution.

Grief doesn't require sameness—it calls for grace.

As grief expert **Kenneth Doka** reminds us:
"We grieve as individuals, but always within a system. To honor grief is to honor difference."

A Lesson from the Past

Part of what helped me hold that perspective was watching what happened in my extended family years earlier.

When my grandfather passed, my aunts and uncles fell into sharp disagreements about how the estate should be handled.

Voices rose in the kitchen, words flung like knives over who was "doing enough" and what was "fair."

What should have been a time of unity unraveled into silence. Siblings who once laughed together now barely spoke. And when my grandmother died years later, the quiet was worse than the arguments. Empty chairs at family gatherings weren't just about who was missing—they were about who chose not to return.

That fracture trickled down to us, the children, who felt the absence like a second loss. I carried that memory with me, determined not to let grief tear my own family apart.

A Brief Chorus of Connection

There were rare moments when, despite our differences, we all seemed to speak the same language.

One evening, after a tense week of small clashes, my siblings and I sat at Mom's kitchen table. Someone retold an old story about my stepfather and his cologne—how he wore it so heavily that you could smell it on the refrigerator door handle or even on food in the fridge, proof he had been there.

Laughter broke out—loud, messy, overlapping.

For a moment, it didn't matter who was cooking, cleaning, or carrying paperwork. We were just children remembering a father-figure we had loved, each in our own way.

It wasn't harmony, not exactly—but it was something like a chorus.

Grieve How You Grieve

You don't have to mimic someone else's process—or silence your own to keep the peace.

Give others room to grieve their way. And protect your own space to grieve your way.

You can't force understanding. But you can set boundaries. You can speak your needs without apology. You can hold space for both connection and disappointment.

And most importantly, you can choose not to let grief become the wedge that divides you.

Practical Anchors: Navigating Family Grief

⇒ **Recognize Roles:** Families fall into roles in grief—the planner, the comforter, the avoider, the over-functioner. None is "right" or "wrong." They're coping strategies.

⇒ **Release Resentment:** Different doesn't mean

absent. Even small gestures are contributions.

⇒ **Draw Boundaries:** Protect your energy without demanding everyone grieve the same way.

⇒ **Find Neutral Ground:** Choose activities or spaces where family can gather without pressure to grieve in unison.

Gentle Scripts

- **To a sibling:** *"I know you're showing up in your own way, and I appreciate that. Here's what would help me right now."*

- **To yourself:** *"Their way doesn't have to match mine for it to matter. Love speaks many languages."*
- **To a parent:** *"I know each of us is grieving differently. Let's give each other space without comparing who's doing it 'right.'"*

Reflection: Navigating Grief in a Family System

Take a steady breath. Let your shoulders drop. Then ask yourself gently:

- Where do I notice differences in how my siblings or family members are grieving?

- How can I remind myself that "different" does not mean "less than"?

- What small step could I take to honor their way, even as I protect my own?

- Where might I need to ask for support—not to change how they grieve, but to share how I'm feeling?

- What compassion can I extend to myself when their style feels far from mine?

- How might these differences reveal new strengths in our family, rather than only tensions?

These aren't questions to grade or solve. They're mirrors, catching you in the raw light of love and difference. Let them guide you toward patience—with your family, and with yourself.

Closing Thought

Grief isn't uniform. It wears many faces, many voices, many silences. Even in a shared loss, your grief remains distinctly yours.

And yet, when woven together, those different languages of sorrow can form something larger than conflict, they can form a chorus. Not always harmonious, sometimes jagged, but always proof that love endures.

Families don't survive by grieving the same way. They survive by listening for the love beneath each language, and choosing to stay at the table—even when the voices sound different.

Because the work isn't to grieve the same. The work is to grieve without fracturing.

Chapter 10
Protecting Your Peace, No Apology Required

"You don't owe anyone your depletion."

T he shadow of boundaries—learning to say no with love, and guarding your own capacity.

I used to think boundaries meant selfishness. But I discovered they are the very thing that makes love sustainable.

Grief has a way of making you a magnet for other people's needs—especially when you're the one who "handles things." The person who always organizes the meal train. The sibling who answers every call. The child who seems "strong enough" to carry the load.

But strength has a cost.

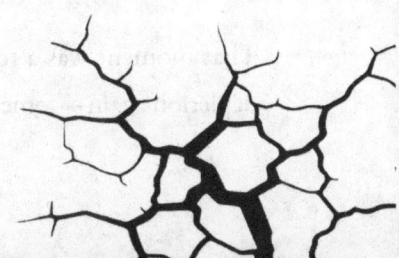

When Superwoman Slips

After my stepfather's passing, what was supposed to be a short visit to support my mom turned into an extended stay. I stepped in quickly, handling estate paperwork, coordinating tasks, keeping things moving so nothing slipped through the cracks.

From the outside, it looked like life was settling into something steady again. The bank accounts were handled. Court papers filed. Mom's days moving in rhythm again.

But inside, I was running on emotional fumes.

When one of my sisters asked for help—ideas for her business, suggestions for home design updates—I felt the old instinct rise up: say yes, figure it out, hold it all together.

Maybe you know this feeling—the weight of saying yes even as your body whispers no.

This time, I listened.

"I just don't have the capacity right now."

The silence after was uncomfortable. But also freeing.

That moment was a revelation. I realized I was defaulting to depletion again—something grief made even harder to recover from. But this time, I chose differently.

The "S" on my chest didn't stand for Superwoman. It stood for sibling. And that was enough.

The Breaking Point

One day, I forgot that lesson. I said yes to too many things at once.

I was working from home on a deadline. I agreed to go to court with my mom for probate paperwork. I added several bank stops. I promised to watch my niece later that evening.

The tasks themselves weren't impossible. But layered together, they became heavy bricks on my chest. By the time I sat back down at my laptop, I could barely breathe under the weight of it all.

The courthouse echo still rang in my ears. Probate papers were still crumpled in my bag. My niece's laughter faded into the background as exhaustion pressed in—and I snapped.

I broke down.

And in that collapse, I realized something had to change.

It wasn't just about being busy. It was about the slow erosion of myself. My mind scattered. My body aching. My spirit thinning out until it felt like I was a shadow in my own life.

That day taught me the importance of pausing before agreeing to anything. Sometimes that meant saying no. Sometimes it meant delaying my answer. Always, it meant protecting the fragile space I needed just to breathe.

I thought every no would come with conflict, maybe even collapse. But then I learned that some no's are softer, almost invisible—and just as powerful.

A Different Kind of No

One evening, a family friend called to ask if Mom and I wanted company for dinner. My instinct was to say yes. That's what I would have done before—welcome them in, fill the house, keep everyone connected.

But I knew Mom was tired. And so was I.

Instead, I answered gently:
   "We love you, but tonight isn't good. Could we plan for another time?"

The relief in my body was immediate.

That "no" wasn't rejection—it was preservation. It gave both Mom and me the gift of quiet.

Boundaries don't always look like confrontation. Sometimes they look like tenderness.

Boundaries Are Not Betrayal

Saying no doesn't make you selfish. It makes you honest.

Grief strips away the extra. What remains should be sacred.

Boundaries aren't walls. They're doors that you get to choose when and how to open. They aren't barriers—they're bridges back to your peace.

> As therapist **Nedra Glover Tawwab** reminds us: "Boundaries are not about keeping others out. They're about keeping yourself whole."

And whole is what you need to be if you're going to hold space for anyone else.

Guilt Will Knock—Don't Let It In

Even when you know the truth, guilt will still show up.

"They need me."

"What if they think I don't care?"

"I owe them."

But guilt isn't a compass. It's a loop. And if you don't

interrupt it, it will drain what little energy you have left.

You don't have to explain your no.

You don't have to justify your quiet.

You don't have to fix what others haven't managed.

Your peace is not a luxury. It's a lifeline.

Practical Anchors: Protecting Your Peace

⇒ **Pause Before Yes:** Ask yourself, *"Do I have the capacity for this?"* before answering.

⇒ **Soft Scripts:**

  ○ *"I want to help, but I don't have the space this week."*

  ○ *"I love you, and the answer is no for now."*

⇒ **Use Delay as Protection:** *"Can I get back to you on that?"* buys time for honesty instead of reflexive yeses.

⇒ **Choose Tender No's:** Declining with love (*"We'd love to see you, but not tonight"*) preserves relationships while guarding energy.

⇒ **Treat Rest as Sacred:** Block time for yourself as if it were an appointment, with no apology.

Reflection: Where Can I Make Space for Myself?

Settle your shoulders. Let the air move slow. Then ask:

- Where in my life do I feel stretched past my true capacity?

- What have I been saying yes to out of guilt rather than alignment?

- What boundary could I set this week that would feel like a breath of relief?

- What part of me needs permission to rest—without apology, without explanation?

- Who or what drains me most—and how might I step back, even a little, without shame?

These aren't rebellions. They're reminders: peace is a lifeline, not a luxury.

Closing Thought

You are not selfish for needing space. You are not weak for saying no.

Every no you honor is a yes to your healing.

You don't have to be everything to everyone. Whole is enough. Whole is powerful. Whole is peace.

And as you practice this, you'll begin to notice something else: protecting your peace not only steadies you—it makes more room for your parent to begin rebuilding theirs.

Because protecting your peace is not just survival—*it's love.*

Part III

Illustration by Mischere V. Kyles

The Long Road of Love

"Grief doesn't end. It changes shape—and so do we."

T he shadows begin to thin, not because the pain is gone, but because light finds new ways to enter.

Eventually, the pies stop and the calls fade. The world expects you "better," but grief doesn't follow a calendar—it follows love.

And when the noise falls quiet, the silence can feel heavier than the storm. This is the long road—not a sprint to "move on," but a winding path you learn to walk. Some days steady. Some days stumbling. Always slower than anyone else imagines.

Along the way, you discover something startling: absence doesn't vanish at milestones. It lingers at weddings, birthdays, holidays, even ordinary Tuesdays. But so does love. The echo of their presence threads through each new beginning, reminding you that grief and love are not opposites, but companions.

If you've ever sat at a holiday table and felt both the ache of who's missing and the warmth of who's present, you already know the tension of this long road.

Part Two showed us how the shadows of grief reshape daily life, how it alters our parents, tests family bonds, and teaches us the quiet strength of boundaries.

Now, Part Three turns toward *living forward*: honoring your parent's becoming, carrying absence into milestones, and redefining what "moving on" really means.

This is the long road—where breaking points become turning points, and where grief shifts from being only an anchor to becoming a teacher.

Here, love takes the lead.

So let's walk this road together. It won't always be easy. But you don't have to walk it alone.

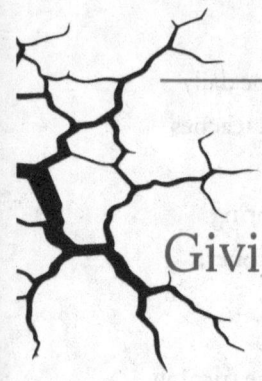

Chapter 11
Giving Yourself Permission to Be Okay

"Healing doesn't mean forgetting. It means remembering without unraveling."

A t first, I believed my parent's grief mattered more than mine. But I learned that my healing deserves permission, too.

Maybe you've felt that tension—the pull to keep everyone else steady while quietly denying your own softness. Once you've made room for peace, the next challenge is believing you're allowed to live in it.

There comes a moment when the heaviness begins to lift. You smile without guilt. You laugh, and it feels real. You go a whole day without crying, and part of you wonders if you should feel bad about that.

You shouldn't.

There's no award for staying broken. You don't owe anyone

your continued suffering.

Sometimes the hardest part after loss isn't grieving—it's giving yourself permission to feel okay again.

What "Okay" Might Look Like

For me, "okay" first showed up in the backyard.

For weeks, I hadn't let myself just be—I was either indoors or running errands, moving from one responsibility to the next. But one afternoon, I finally sat outside, in the sunlight, on my stepfather's old blue chair.

At first, that chair had been unbearable to look at. But this time, I sat. The fabric was sun-faded, the metal arms cool against my skin. My niece ran out with a soccer ball, her laughter spilling across the yard.

We kicked the ball back and forth, missing more shots than we made, until we were laughing so hard it felt almost foreign in my own chest.

That moment didn't erase grief—it widened the room so life could walk back in.

When Laughter Returns

Months later, during a family gathering, someone cracked a

spiraling joke that left everyone doubled over, wiping tears from their eyes.

For the first time since his passing, I laughed without holding back.

It didn't feel like betrayal. It felt like love stretching wide enough to hold both laughter and loss.

That's what healing looks like—not erasure, but expansion.

Planning Forward Without Guilt

As time passed, my mom and I began planning again—bowling tournaments, road trips, ordinary joys that once felt impossible.

At first, even the idea felt like a theft, as though moving forward meant leaving him behind. But we came to see it differently. Each plan wasn't erasure—it was continuation. A quiet way of saying: life is still here.

For me, that meant daring to plan again, booking a simple trip to what I call my "slice of paradise." Sitting near the water, listening to waves roll against the shore, I realized peace didn't betray him. It carried him forward.

Why Permission Feels Hard

Part of why joy feels dangerous isn't just personal—it's cultural. Some communities equate solemnity with love: the longer you wear grief visibly, the more it proves your devotion. Others quietly pressure you to "move on," equating laughter with closure. Both miss the truth: healing is not a performance.

We know from other traditions and cultures around the globe that grief and celebration are not opposites—they are kin. They teach us that honoring a life doesn't always require silence; sometimes, it requires color, music, and laughter to fully hold a person's memory. If entire cultures can hold that paradox, maybe we can too.

Expert Insight

Psychologist **George Bonanno** has studied grief resilience for decades. His findings are startling: most people adapt more quickly than they expect. Joy isn't the exception—it's the norm.

And **Elisabeth Kübler-Ross** herself clarified that her famous "stages" were never meant as a rigid path:

> "Grief is as individual as love itself."

Your laughter, your trip, your coffee shared with a friend—

these are not betrayals. They are proof you're carrying love differently now.

Practical Anchors: Permission to Be Okay

⇒ **Notice the Shift:** Pay attention when joy sneaks in—a smile, a rest, a laugh.

⇒ **Challenge Guilt:** Replace "I shouldn't" with "I'm allowed."

⇒ **Re-enter Slowly:** Let joy come in small steps.

⇒ **Celebrate Ordinary:** Healing often shows up in everyday tasks—cooking, walking, resting.

⇒ **Speak It Out Loud:** Tell someone about a joy you've allowed back in. Naming it makes it real.

Reflection: What Am I Ready to Receive Again?

Place your hand on your chest. Feel its rhythm. Then reflect:

• Where have I been keeping life at a distance, afraid it would erase my grief?

• Where am I noticing sparks of lightness, even if fleeting?

- How might joy coexist with memory, instead of competing with it?

- Who in my circle makes space for both my sorrow and my laughter—without judgment?

- What joy am I ready to allow back into my days without apology?

These aren't signs of forgetting—they're gestures of grace, allowing life and love to weave together again.

Closing Thought

There's no timeline for being okay—and no shame in arriving there.

Grief changes you, but it doesn't cancel your capacity for life.

Let the joy in—without apology. Let the light back through.

You don't have to prove your pain. You only have to honor your healing.

Being okay isn't forgetting—it's carrying love with more room for joy.

And when you give yourself that permission, you quietly give your parent permission too—to keep living, to keep becoming.

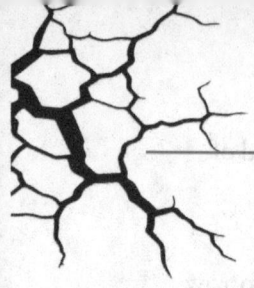

Chapter 12
Witnessing the Becoming

"We mourn who they were, even as we walk beside who they are becoming."

W hat I didn't expect was that grief would not only change my parent's story, but reveal new chapters of their becoming—and mine.

When a parent loses their spouse, the loss ripples outward. You don't just grieve the partner they've lost—you begin to grieve the version of them that may never fully return.

They may pause longer before answering. Their laughter may take longer to rise. Their movements may slow, their routines unravel, their sharpness dim. It's not just that their spouse is missing—it's that a part of them has shifted, too.

And yet, in the midst of those changes, something else stirs. A new version of them begins to take shape—sometimes fragile, sometimes strong, often unpredictable.

Your task is not to force them back into who they were, but to walk with them as they slowly become who they are now. To honor the partner they lost while making space for the parent

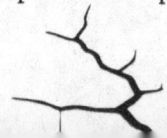

who is still here—different, but not gone.

I saw this unfolding slowly in my own home.

The Weight of the Unknown

In the early months, my mother often whispered, eyes down on the paperwork:
"I don't even know where to begin."

It wasn't just about bills. It was about life itself. Without her partner, every choice felt uncertain—like stepping into a room where the furniture had been rearranged in the dark.

What once was automatic now carried hesitation. Even the simplest routines asked new questions:
Do I do this alone?
Do I still do this at all?

I responded with patience—at first. But as weeks stretched into months, that patience thinned. Inside, I found myself thinking:
Are we still here? Still circling the same questions?

There were days she surprised me—getting up early, heading to the gym, making plans to rebuild strength. And then there were days she stayed in bed, or sat by the window for hours, staring at the world outside but not entering it.

What looked like setbacks tested my resolve. Until I realized: grief isn't linear. Rebuilding isn't a straight staircase. It's one step, then stillness. Progress, then fog. And that too was part of the becoming.

The Fog of Grief

Grief is not always about doing. Sometimes, it's about sitting in the fog before the next step appears.

Like clothes that hang untouched in the closet, waiting for the day you feel ready to decide whether to keep, donate, or pass them on.

Like the unopened mail on the counter, or the quiet ritual of sitting in the same chair again and again, not because it's productive, but because it anchors you when everything else feels unsteady.

I came to understand: those pauses weren't setbacks. They were processing—the human work of absorbing change.

It was okay to just be. And oddly, it was that grace—the permission to sit without rushing—that gave us the foundation to keep going when the fog finally lifted.

Rebuilding Together

Grief doesn't only unravel—it reshapes.

For my mother, rebuilding began with bowling tournaments. She had always traveled with my stepfather for competitions, and after his passing, she hesitated. Going back felt impossible. But one year, she chose to attend.

This time, I carried the bags, checked the equipment, and made sure logistics were in order. It wasn't about her standing alone—not yet. It was about us learning a new rhythm together.

She bowled one of her best games in years—not because the grief was gone, but because she dared to live inside it.

Other rebuilding moments were quieter. Like the morning I watched her make coffee again after months of avoiding it. It wasn't just a cup of coffee. It was a reclamation. A whisper: *I am still here.*

The Stage She Stepped Onto

And then there was the theatre.

Nights had become especially heavy without my stepfather. So, when my mother signed up to volunteer at a local playhouse, as a hostess for productions coming through the city—it caught us by surprise.

At first, we, her children, were apprehensive. This was something she would do on her own, often at night, and it was unfamiliar territory. Part of us wanted to keep her close, to pull back the reins. But another part knew we had to let her step forward into this new chapter.

She went to the first meeting nervous but determined. When she came home, her eyes carried a brightness we hadn't seen in months. She spoke with excitement about meeting new people, about the thrill of trying something different, about how good it felt to be part of a community again.

It wasn't about the plays themselves—it was about possibility. About rediscovering independence, joy, and connection.

Maybe you've watched this too—the quiet courage of a parent daring to begin again, even when the world still feels half-lit.

Watching her, I realized: rebuilding doesn't always mean returning to the old. Sometimes it looks like stepping onto an entirely new stage—one where grief still walks with you, but so does hope.

Expert Insight

> As **Pauline Boss**, who coined the term *ambiguous loss*, reminds us: "Loss is not always about what is gone, but about learning to live with what has changed."

Your parent's becoming is not a betrayal of who they were. It is the only way forward.

Practical Anchors: Walking Beside the Becoming

⇒ **Notice Without Forcing:** Observe shifts in your parent's energy, routines, or moods without pressuring them to "return" to their old self.

⇒ **Honor the Still Days:** Quiet isn't a setback— it's part of the rhythm of rebuilding. Stillness holds its own kind of strength.

⇒ **Encourage Gently:** Offer invitations, not ultimatums. "Would you like me to join you for a walk?" carries more grace than *"You should get out more."*

⇒ **Celebrate Small Restorations:** Making coffee, attending a tournament, volunteering at a playhouse, acknowledge these as victories, however ordinary they may seem.

Reflection: Who Is My Parent Becoming?

Take a steadying breath. Settle into the stillness. Let these questions open gently, like doors you don't have to rush through:

• What parts of my parent feel unfamiliar now—and

how might they be signs of who they are becoming, rather than only what's been lost?

- Where do I catch glimpses of resilience, even if small— an everyday act that hints at their strength returning?

- How can I stand beside them in ways that steady, but do not control?

- What version of them am I clinging to—and what would it mean to release that version while still honoring their essence?

These aren't questions to fix. They are invitations—to notice, to soften, to expand the lens through which you see both your parent and yourself. Grief reshapes slowly. The witnessing is part of the love.

Closing Thought

Your parent's grief will reshape them, but it does not erase them.

Hold space for who they were. Hold hope for who they are becoming.

Because love doesn't cling only to the past—it also sows seeds for the future.

(pause)

And sometimes, the greatest gift you can give is not to demand the return of who they once were, but to stand beside them long enough to watch who they are becoming.

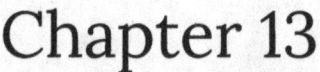

Chapter 13
When the Support Ends and the Silence Echoes

"The Cards Stop. The Calls Fade. And Suddenly, It's Just You and the Quiet."

I thought the hardest part was the funeral. But the real ache came later, when the support faded and silence grew loud.

Part Three began with this truth: eventually, the visitors leave, the doorbell stops ringing, and the quiet feels louder than the noise ever did.

In the early days, people show up. Meals are delivered. Flowers arrive. Calls pour in. For a while, you feel surrounded, held in a circle of care.

Then slowly, the circle thins. The meals stop. The texts grow quiet. The rhythm of support fades—sometimes all at once. And you're left wondering how the world moved on so quickly when yours still hasn't.

When the Crowd Fades

I remember when the meals stopped. In the beginning, there was always something warm on the stove—brought by a sibling, a neighbor, an aunt or uncle, even a cousin dropping by with a dish. The house felt full, even if we were all grieving.

My siblings pitched in with cooking, cleaning, planning outings, checking in on our mom. Extended family offered their own kind of presence, stories at the table, extra chairs filled, reminders that we weren't alone. Each of us showed up in our own way.

But as days turned into weeks, people naturally returned to their routines. The steady support that had wrapped around us grew thinner. My siblings and relatives meant no harm; they were simply moving back into their lives.

Still, when the last dish left the table and the door closed behind them, the quiet felt heavier than I expected.

The Queen Chair

In that season, my mother often retreated to her floral queen chair tucked inside her bedroom suite.
That chair wasn't just furniture—it became her throne of resilience.

Some evenings she was fully engaged, watching her favorite

westerns or humming along with an old radio station. Other times, she drifted into silence, her head tilted gently to the side as she slept, the lamp beside her casting a soft glow.

At first, I tried to manage her time there—suggesting she do something different, nudging her toward activity. But eventually I realized: this was her story to author. My role wasn't to dictate her grief, but to honor her space within it.

That shift changed me. If she needed stillness, I gave her stillness. If she needed presence, I sat nearby. Love, not correction, became my posture.

That chair taught me something no book could: grief isn't to be fixed—it's to be honored.

Grief Doesn't Follow Their Timeline

Family therapist **Pauline Boss** calls this *ambiguous loss*—when someone is physically present but emotionally altered, or when grief continues long after the visible rituals have ended.

The fading of visible support doesn't mean grief has ended. As Boss reminds us: *"The world may move on, but your inner world needs more time."*

The problem isn't that others stop caring. It's that they stop remembering.

They assume you're back to normal. They assume you've moved on. Or maybe it's just easier for them to look away.

But grief isn't a moment—it's a migration.

When others retreat, your process can feel invisible. That's why this part of the journey often feels the loneliest: because the outside world no longer mirrors the ache inside.

And here's the truth: if others fade, it doesn't mean your grief is wrong. It only means their timeline is different from yours. Healing takes as long as it takes, and yours will not match theirs.

Rebuilding Support on Your Terms

Silence isn't your fault. It isn't proof that your grief is too much, or that their love was too little. It's simply how life moves—faster for others than your healing can keep up.

But you don't have to grieve in isolation. You can rebuild support on your own terms. That might look like:

➤ Letting one trusted person know: *"I'm still not okay."*
➤ Starting a small ritual to honor your loved one.
➤ Joining a grief group or faith community.
➤ Writing, creating, or walking as forms of release.
➤ Asking siblings, friends, or family for specific commitments: a weekly call, a dinner, a shared check-in.
➤ Gently reminding others: "My grief didn't end when the funeral did."

Support may not look like it did in the beginning—but that

doesn't mean it's gone.

Sometimes you have to invite it back. And sometimes, you discover new forms of support that feel lighter, steadier, and more sustainable than before.

Reflection: What Do I Need Now?

Take a breath. Let the quiet around you settle. Then reflect slowly:

- Where do I feel the deepest silence—in my home, my relationships, or within myself?

- When support faded, what did I miss most: the practical help, the conversations, or simply the reminder that others remembered I was still grieving?

- Who in my circle can I be honest with about my ongoing grief—and what would it look like to invite them back into my support system?

- What request for support have I been afraid to make—and what might change if I voiced it gently?

- How do I care for myself when others are not present—what rituals, spaces, or practices remind me

I am still held?

- How can I learn to see silence not only as emptiness, but also as space for rest, memory, or renewal?

These aren't questions to fix overnight. They are pathways back to remembering that even in silence, your story—and your needs—still matter.

Closing Thought

The silence may feel hollow—but it is also space.

Space for remembering. Space for release. Space for rebuilding.

That floral queen chair became more than a seat for my mother. It became a reminder that even in quiet, there is presence. Even in stillness, there is story.

The world may grow quiet around you, but you are not forgotten. You are still held—in memory, in community, and in love that continues forward.

In time, we would each return to our own rhythms—me to my home, my mother to her quiet rituals—but in those early months, we were still learning how to let the silence hold us, together.

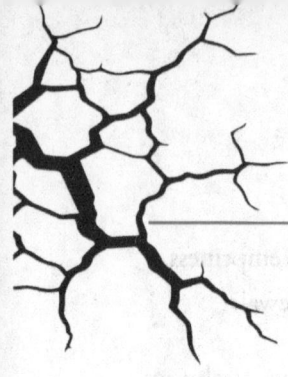

Chapter 14
When Their Absence Meets Your Milestones

"The celebration doesn't erase the sorrow—it carries it."

A t first, I believed milestones would only be lonely. But I discovered they can also become spaces where legacy shows up most clearly.

After the visitors leave and the doorbell stops ringing, silence takes on new shapes. One of the loudest is at milestones.

Graduations. Birthdays. Holidays. Promotions. Weddings.

These are the moments when absence feels sharpest—not only because they're missing, but because you imagine their reaction.
The call you would've gotten. The outfit they would've worn. The way they would've clapped, laughed, or made the moment bigger.

Instead, you carry their memory quietly, behind your smile.

You clap for yourself, knowing they would have. But the ache still pulses underneath the joy.

When the Table Feels Different

For the first time, we planned my parents' wedding anniversary without him. My siblings and I wanted to be sure our mother didn't face the day alone, so we gathered for dinner.

At first, it felt almost ordinary—menus in hand, chatter around the table. But then came the pause. We were so used to watching him order his favorite steak, always with ketchup instead of steak sauce, and his drink, requested with a grin. This time, no order came.

I looked at my mother then. Her smile was steady, but her eyes softened, and in that small silence I felt the weight of his absence more than in any empty chair.

The food was the same, the laughter familiar—but the table felt altered, reshaped. Even joy came with echoes.

Grief had pulled up its own chair, quiet but present, reminding us that every celebration now carried two truths: who was missing and how love still found a way to stay.

Roses on the Table

That year, we also brought roses to the celebration—pink, in honor of their love. Normally, roses last only two or three weeks. But these lingered, blooming for nearly eight. Their edges browned, but they refused to fade.

Every time we walked past them, they seemed to whisper what my mother put into words:

> "It's like he's saying love will continue to grow despite the transition."

Those roses became more than flowers. They became a symbol—that love doesn't end when life does. It stretches, it adapts, it endures.

Celebrating in Layers

Milestones become mosaics of emotion. Joy sits beside sorrow. Pride walks hand-in-hand with longing.

You may find yourself smiling in one moment and tearing up in the next. That's not a contradiction—it's a full-hearted experience.

You're not doing it wrong because you miss them. You're doing it bravely because you're still moving forward.

Making Space for Their Spirit

There are ways to bring them with you—not to replace the absence, but to honor their place in your story.

Maybe it's lighting a candle at your graduation. Wearing

something they gave you on your birthday. Cooking their favorite dish at the holidays.

Maybe it's saving them a seat—not literally, but in the way you share a story about them before the toast.

These gestures say: *You mattered. You still do.*

Expert Insight

Researcher **William Worden**, known for his *Tasks of Mourning*, describes one of grief's essential movements as *"finding an enduring connection with the deceased while embarking on a new life."*

That's what milestones ask of us—not to deny the absence, but to weave the memory into the present.

Your tears at the wedding, your smile at graduation, your candle at the holiday table—these are all ways of carrying that enduring connection forward.

Practical Anchors: Carrying Them Into Your Milestones

⇒ **Mark the Day:** Create a ritual when milestones arrive—a prayer, a toast, a candle, a story.

⇒ **Share Their Legacy:** Invite others to name a favorite memory at the gathering.

⇒ **Carry a Token:** Wear their jewelry, carry their handkerchief, slip a note in your pocket.

⇒ **Blend Joy and Grief:** Let yourself cry and celebrate. Both belong.

⇒ **Choose Continuity:** Keep one tradition they loved, while starting a new one that reflects life now.

⇒ **Gentle Script:** Whisper to yourself, "I wish you were here. I'm carrying you with me today."

Reflection: How Can I Include Them in What's Ahead?

Settle your shoulders. Breathe slow. Then let these questions meet you where you are:

- If they were here, how would they have celebrated me—what words, what gestures, what presence?

- Where can I honor that spirit in my own way? A candle? A toast? A whispered thank you?

- What permission do I need to give myself—to feel joy, to laugh, to plan—without guilt?

- How might I invite others into remembering, so I don't carry the silence alone?

- What tradition could I begin now, one that honors them each time a milestone arrives, so love has a place to land?

These aren't assignments to check off. They are invitations—to carry both absence and presence into the life that keeps unfolding.

Closing Thought

You're allowed to feel it all. To cry and dance. To miss them and celebrate yourself.

Their absence may echo. But your joy still matters.

Because love, even after loss, finds its way into every milestone you reach. Like those pink roses, it may change form, but it will keep blooming—quietly, steadily, against all odds.

The silence that once held only ache now holds remembrance.

And when you allow space for both, you honor not only their memory but also your own becoming.

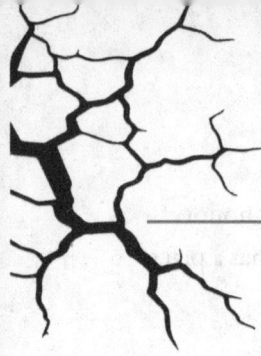

Chapter 15
What Moving On Really Looks Like

"You don't move on. You move forward—with what remains."

I once assumed moving on meant leaving them behind. But I learned it's about carrying them differently—into the life you're still building.

Silence comes in many forms. It lingers in the home, it alters milestones—and eventually, it settles in when the visitors leave and the doorbell stops ringing. And in that quiet, another question begins to surface: *When will you move on?*

Grief comes with a quiet pressure—the unspoken expectation that, eventually, you'll be "better." Back to normal. Past the sadness. Done.

But grief doesn't work like that. It's not a finish line. It's a companion that keeps changing form.

To "move on" sounds like leaving something behind. But you haven't left them behind. You've carried them with you—through the breakdowns and breakthroughs, the hard decisions and quiet victories.

Moving forward doesn't mean forgetting. It means adapting—with love, not absence.

As grief expert **David Kessler** reminds us:

> "We don't move on from grief. We move forward with it."

His insight reframes healing—not as disloyalty, but as proof of the depth of the bond we carry forward.

What Forward Might Look Like

You start making plans again. You set boundaries. You smile more often than you cry. You discover parts of yourself that grief uncovered.

You realize you can hold space for sadness and still crave life.

This is growth—not abandonment.

I remember when my mother and I began to smile more. There were lighter moments, even laughter. Someone remarked on how well she seemed to be doing—implying she must be "over it."

Later, she pulled me aside, her voice steady but firm:

> "My children have been a gift in my grief. Your support has helped me breathe again. But being in better spirits doesn't mean I'm over my husband's loss."

That moment stayed with me. Healing isn't a departure from love—it's an extension of it.

Maybe you've felt it too—the tug-of-war between remembering and rebuilding. That quiet guilt when joy returns sooner than expected.

You are not betraying their memory by healing. You are honoring their impact by continuing.

A Subtle Example of Forward

Bowling had been a thread running through my mother's life with my stepfather. Together, they traveled for tournaments, bowled in leagues, and built friendships at the lanes.

After his passing, she couldn't bear it. Invitations from friends to return only deepened the ache. The sound of pins crashing felt too hollow without him. The smell of polished lanes, the rhythm of shoes sliding across wood—these were no longer simple rituals. They had become reminders.

But slowly, she eased back in. At first, I carried the bags, checked equipment, made sure logistics were in order. She was stepping forward, but not yet alone.

And then came the day she drove herself. She signed up for her leagues again. She practiced on her own. She walked back into the lanes—not to erase grief, but to live with it.

What struck me most wasn't just the act of bowling. It was her presence—confident, independent, even willing to answer the tender questions about my stepfather without shrinking back.

In different ways, both bowling and baseball taught her the same truth: the world didn't stop turning when grief arrived, and she didn't have to stop living to honor who she lost.

Months after his passing, when baseball season began, she decided to go to a game. For years, she was the one who purchased the tickets, while my stepfather handled the driving—making sure she was dropped off safely before heading inside together.

This time, that safety net was gone. She opened the stadium app on her phone, had her ticket scanned by the usher, and found her seat on her own. The sound of the crowd swelled around her—the crack of the bat, the hum of voices, the anthem echoing across the field.

From where I sat, I could see her take it all in—steady, composed, quietly brave.

She wasn't moving on from him. She was moving forward *with* him.

To anyone else, these might have looked like ordinary outings. But to us, they carried the weight of survival and the light of resilience.

Forward doesn't erase what was. It makes space for what still can be.

Letting the Phrase Evolve

Maybe "moving on" never felt right. That's okay.

Try reframing:

- "I'm moving with my grief, not past it."

- "I'm rebuilding with what they gave me."

- "I'm still becoming, even as I remember."

Let your language evolve with your healing. Let your story hold space for all of it.

Practical Anchors: Living Forward Without Leaving Behind

⇒ **Name the Growth:** Notice one part of yourself that has expanded since the loss—resilience, empathy, patience.

⇒ **Mark Gentle Firsts:** A first holiday, trip, or gathering can feel raw. Choose one ritual to honor their presence while embracing your new experience.

⇒ **Honor the Return of Tears:** Tears after months of progress aren't regressions; they're reminders that love still lives.

⇒ **Invite Life In:** Say yes to something small—a walk, a project, a dinner. Let life return without demanding it erase grief.

⇒ **Carry Tokens:** A phrase, photo, or tradition can travel with you into new spaces. You don't leave them—you bring them.

⇒ **Share Your Language:** Tell someone close: "Forward doesn't mean I'm over it—it means I'm carrying them as I go."

Reflection: What Does Moving Forward Look Like for Me?

Take a breath. Feel your feet steady against the floor. Let these questions open softly:

- What messages about "moving on" have I absorbed—from culture, family, or community— that don't fit my reality?

- In what small ways has grief changed me—and how can I honor that growth instead of fearing it?

- What part of my life am I ready to reimagine, not erase?

- How do I want to carry their presence into new milestones or seasons ahead?

- What does "forward" mean to me today—and how might that meaning change tomorrow?

These aren't questions for closure. They are invitations to walk gently, with love as your compass.

Closing Thought

You don't have to move on. You only have to move honestly.

With your grief. With your growth. With your memories.

You're still becoming. And that, too, is love.

And as you move forward, you show your parent—*and yourself—that healing isn't leaving. It's carrying.*

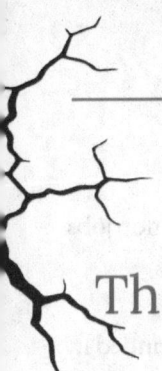

Chapter 16
The Role You Never Asked For

"I didn't choose this role. But I can choose how I carry it."

I thought roles were chosen.

But some are handed to us without warning—and our strength is found not in refusing them, but in how we carry them.

Loss doesn't just take away. It redistributes.

When a parent loses their spouse, responsibilities shift like tectonic plates—sometimes suddenly, sometimes slowly, but always in ways you feel.

Suddenly, you may be:

- The one who drives them to appointments.

- The one who manages the bills or estate paperwork.

- The one who becomes the voice at family gatherings, smoothing over tension.

- The one who answers their late-night calls when the

silence feels too heavy.

These roles arrive without permission slips. They're not jobs you signed up for.

And yet, here you are, holding them, because love demanded it.

The Uninvited Mantle

I remember sitting at the kitchen table after my stepfather's passing, papers spread around us like puzzle pieces. My mother had always leaned on him for balance when it came to financial matters. Suddenly, I became that balance.

It wasn't a conversation we planned. It wasn't a title I accepted. It simply happened—by proximity, by necessity, by love.

But with it came a quiet tension: How do you support without suffocating? Lead without erasing? Carry without collapsing?

The role wasn't chosen. It was inherited—like a heavy coat draped across my shoulders before I had the chance to prepare.

When Roles Collide

Taking on new responsibilities after loss often collides with old family patterns.

Maybe you're the sibling who always handled details—so naturally, everyone looks to you. Maybe you're the one who lives closest, so proximity decides for you. Or maybe you're the "responsible one," the one others assume will manage things.

Those assumptions can create friction. What feels like duty to one person can feel like absence to another.

In my own family, I noticed this when estate matters arose. I stepped in to make sure nothing slipped through the cracks— court dates, probate paperwork, financial accounts. Meanwhile, others helped in quieter ways: meals, a clean kitchen, a drive across town.

At first, I compared. I measured. I resented. I told myself I was carrying the heavier load.

But grief is a harsh teacher. It reminded me that my role didn't make me the hero, and their roles didn't make them absent. We were all fumbling toward care in the only ways we knew how.

The Day the Roles Reversed

One afternoon, not long after my stepfather's passing, I drove my mom to a doctor's appointment—something he had always done.

That day, I found myself in his seat.

I listened as the doctor spoke, taking notes while my mom sat quietly, overwhelmed by the swirl of medical terms. At one point, she turned to me with eyes that seemed to ask, *"What do I do now?"*

The weight of that moment sank deep: I wasn't just her daughter. I was stepping into the role of her advocate, her protector, her anchor.

And it didn't stop there.

Soon, I was also sitting beside her at financial planning meetings, scanning documents, researching policy terms, and calling companies to confirm details. My stepfather had always been the one to handle home repairs, meet contractors, or manage insurance questions. Now, those responsibilities flowed my way.

At first, I felt unprepared—like a student suddenly asked to teach the class. But over time, I learned to navigate the rhythm. I'd schedule appointments, gather quotes, review fine print, and explain options back to her in plain language. Slowly, my mother began to look to me the way she once looked to him— not because she couldn't manage, but because I had become her bridge to the unfamiliar.

And though the work was demanding, something shifted: I started finding balance.

Where I once reacted out of urgency, I began responding with steadiness. Where I once carried alone, I began to collaborate— with her, not just for her.

Grief, it turns out, doesn't just reshape relationships through emotion. It also rearranges who handles the paperwork, who answers the questions, who steadies the home.

And somewhere between scanning documents and scheduling repairs, I found a new kind of rhythm—one that honored both her rebuilding and my boundaries.

The Weight of Expectation

Taking on this role can feel like an invisible weight.

You may feel responsible for your parent's healing.
You may feel guilty for needing space of your own.
You may feel like no one notices the load you're carrying.

And all the while, the world claps for you—the "strong one," the "dutiful child."
But the applause doesn't lighten the weight. Sometimes, it only makes it heavier.

The truth is: you didn't ask for this role.
But you can choose how you inhabit it.

Not as a martyr. Not as the only one holding it all together. But as someone learning to balance love with limits.

The Grief of the Mantle

Taking on this mantle carried its own quiet grief.

Deep down, I felt myself moving up in the unspoken order—

the one others begin to look to for steadiness. My grandparents were gone. Aunts and uncles had passed. Now the weight of being the anchor began to settle on me.

There's a strange ache in realizing you are the one others will call first, lean on most, depend upon quietly.
 It's not a role you prepare for—it's one you inherit.

And with it comes both strength and sorrow: pride in what you can carry, grief for the innocence of no longer being the one cared for.

If you've ever felt yourself becoming the one others look to, you know this paradox.
It humbles you and weighs on you at once.

It's both a mantle of love and a reminder of all that has shifted.

Choosing Agency in the Unchosen

You didn't choose this role, but you can choose how you carry it:

⇒ **Name It:** Say out loud, *"I didn't choose this, but I am choosing how I respond."* Naming breaks the illusion that duty is destiny.

⇒ **Share It:** Invite siblings, cousins, or close friends to carry pieces with you. A check-in call, a grocery run, or simply visiting can redistribute the weight.

⇒ **Redefine It:** You're not your parent's savior. You're their support. That distinction frees you from impossible expectations.

⇒ **Release It:** Some responsibilities don't belong to you. Hand back what isn't yours, even if it feels awkward.

⇒ **Communicate Clearly:** Tell your parent gently, *"I'll help with this part, but I can't do everything."* Boundaries are not abandonment—they are honesty.

Reflection: The Role I Never Asked For

Take a breath. Place your hand on your chest. Ask yourself gently:

- What role did I step into after the loss that I never asked for?

- Which of those responsibilities feel heavy—and which feel meaningful?

- Where have I been carrying out of fear, guilt, or expectation rather than love?

- Who can I invite to share one small piece of this load?

143

- How might I honor my parent while still protecting my own becoming?

- In what ways have I become the "parent" in moments where I used to be the child—and how do I feel about that shift?

These aren't questions of blame. They are questions of balance—reminders that you're not only a caretaker, but also a human being with needs of your own.

Closing Thought

The role you never asked for may never feel natural.
But it doesn't have to undo you.

You can carry it differently. With limits. With honesty.
With a posture that says: *"I am here, but I am still me."*

Because love doesn't demand your depletion.
It only asks for your presence.

And sometimes, the greatest gift you can give your parent isn't perfection—it's the courage to stand beside them without losing yourself in the process.

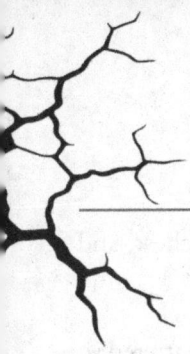

Chapter 17
What Grief Taught Me About Love

"Grief is the proof of love's depth."

A t first, I believed grief was the enemy. But I learned it was only proof of how deeply I had loved—and still do.

If grief is the shadow, then love is the light that casts it.

We often think of grief as a thief—the thing that steals breath, empties rooms, and rearranges lives. But grief only exists because love was here first. The ache you feel is the echo of devotion. The tears you shed are evidence of a bond that shaped you.

Grief, in its own way, is love persevering.

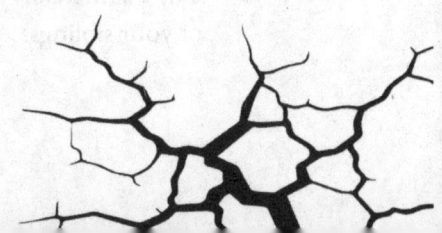

Love Shows Up in the Ache

There are nights when silence presses against your chest, and every inhale feels weighted with memory.

That ache is love's residue. It means their presence mattered so deeply that their absence still rearranges the air you breathe.

When I look back on my stepfathers' lives, I remember their quirks, their humor, their habits—the crosswords and riddles, the long afternoons at the bowling alley, the smoke curling up from the grill. Those ordinary rhythms became sacred in their absence.

It was grief that sharpened my awareness, teaching me that love isn't found only in grand gestures—it lives in the quiet consistencies we once took for granted.

Love in What's Left Behind

After my stepfather passed, I often found my mother lingering near his desk, her hand tracing the wood as though it might still answer her touch. She didn't need words. That gesture alone was a conversation between love and loss.

By now, I'd come to recognize grief's quiet rhythm: it teaches you to notice what remains.

- The hat still hanging by the door.
- The song that stops you mid-aisle.
- The mannerisms you suddenly recognize in yourself or your siblings.

These remnants don't erase the loss—but they remind you that love leaves fingerprints everywhere.

Love Expands When Tested

I once thought love was strongest when life was whole. But grief revealed its truest strength when life broke apart.

In my family, love became practical rides to appointments, meals on the table, hands sorting through paperwork. It became patient listening to my mother repeat questions, holding her silence without rushing her forward. It became fierce protecting her from comments that dismissed her pain.

Love stretched beyond convenience. It became commitment.

And in that stretching, I discovered something else: grief doesn't just teach you about the love you lost. It deepens the love you have left.

That same love reshaped my family—and the way I show up for others

Love Deepens Empathy

One of my closest friends lost both her mother and her father. I had always cared for her pain, but only after walking my own road of loss did I truly begin to understand the weight she carried.

Before, I offered comfort. After, I offered presence.

I didn't try to fix her pain. I simply sat in it with her.

She didn't need explanations, she just needed someone who knew.

That's what grief does, it forges empathy into something sacred. It moves you from sympathy to solidarity.

The Paradox of Love and Grief

Here's the paradox: the more deeply you love, the more deeply you grieve. And yet, it's that very love that gives you the strength to endure the grief.

It's like standing at the shoreline—pain pulls you under, but love keeps you afloat. You rise, sputtering but breathing, because love anchors you even when loss tries to undo you.

As writer **Jamie Anderson** once said:

> "Grief, I've learned, is really just love. It's all the love you want to give but cannot. All of that unspent love gathers in the corners of your eyes, the lump in your throat, and the hollow of your chest."

Grief doesn't destroy love. It redirects it.

Love Becomes Legacy

Perhaps the greatest lesson grief offers is this: love doesn't end with death.

It continues in the way you cook their favorite dish, the way you laugh at their old jokes, the way you tell their stories to the next generation.

It lives in the boundaries you now protect, in the compassion you extend to others, in the strength you've uncovered within yourself.

In my family, it shows up in the rhythms that remain—the lanes where my mother still bowls, the baseball games she now drives herself to, the riddles and puzzles we still pass down.

Love becomes legacy—not because you force it, but because it refuses to leave.

Practical Anchors: Letting Love Lead the Grief

⇒ **Name the Love Beneath the Ache:** When the tears come, whisper: *This hurts because I loved deeply.*

⇒ **Notice the Fingerprints:** Write down the quirks, habits, or sayings that still surface. These are love's echoes.

⇒ **Practice Love-in-Action:** Cook a recipe, play their song, teach a child something they once taught you.

⇒ **Expand Love's Reach:** Let grief soften your compassion toward others.

⇒ **Reframe the Weight:** Instead of asking *When will this grief end?* try *How is love still alive in me through this grief?*

Reflection: Lessons of Love

Take a steady breath. Let your shoulders drop. Then ask yourself gently:

- Where has grief revealed just how deeply I loved?

- What everyday spaces, objects, or moments still carry their presence?

- How has my love shifted form—showing up now in care for my parent, or tenderness toward myself?

- When has grief expanded my capacity to love others more fully, even in small ways?

- What pieces of their love do I long to carry forward into my own story and legacy?

These aren't demands for answers. They're invitations—to notice how love, even in grief, keeps reshaping you: quietly, steadily, endlessly.

Closing Thought

Grief is not love's opposite. It is love's proof.

Every ache, every tear, every pause in the middle of the day is evidence that what you shared mattered—and still does.

What grief taught me about love is simple, but profound: Love does not end. It reshapes. It lingers.

It is our enduring connection, and in the end, it's love that keeps you steady enough to carry the grief... the one thing strong enough to hold both memory and becoming.

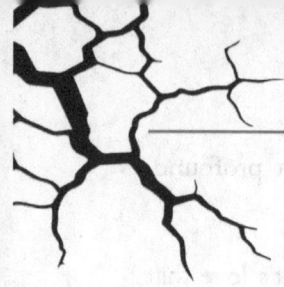

Chapter 18
Life After the Breaking Point

"Healing doesn't mean forgetting. It means remembering without fear."

I once assumed healing meant moving past the pain. But I discovered it means learning to live with both, the ache and the joy—without fear.

There comes a moment—often later than you expect—when the question shifts from, *"How do I survive this?"* to *"What do I do with all of this now?"*
Grief, in all its weight, reshapes us. But so does resilience.

Somewhere along the way, the days begin to feel less heavy. You may laugh without guilt.

You may make plans for the future without apology. You may even find yourself reaching for joy—not as a betrayal of the person you lost, but as a way to honor them.

This is not forgetting. This is integrating.

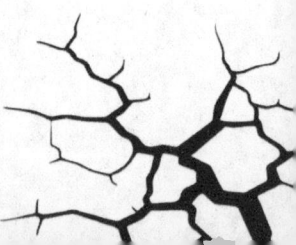

Healing isn't about moving on; it's about moving forward *with*.

The memories come with you. The lessons come with you. I wasn't leaving him behind; I was rebuilding with what remains, a life I was still shaping.

A quiet companion. A reminder. A teacher. Some days it whispers. Other days it roars. But it no longer paralyzes.

That, too, is healing.

Letting the Future Be Yours Again

There's a strange permission you have to give yourself after a loss—the permission to live.

To enjoy holidays. To plan new traditions. To laugh deeply. To love fiercely.

For me, that looked like saying yes to things I once felt guilty about: traveling again, joining family outings, even moments of lightness with friends.

I remember one evening, months after my stepfather's passing, when laughter surprised me. It burst out mid-conversation, unplanned and unguarded. And then it startled me—like I had broken some unspoken rule.

But instead of guilt, I chose grace. I reminded myself: joy didn't erase the grief. It simply added dimension to it.

I wasn't leaving him behind. I was bringing him forward—into the life I was still building.

Grief carves you open. But it also carves space for new things. And though life is different now, it is still yours to shape.

Returning Home

The day finally came for me to return home. After six months away, I felt both relief and fear—relief that I could reclaim my own rhythm, fear of how my mother and I would do without each other.

We created a system of communication that felt strong.

One night she called me and said quietly, *"I'm crying. I miss him."*
I gave her space and said, "Mom, allow yourself to feel his loss. Go take a sip of his favorite beer, listen to his song, whisper to him how you miss him—in your way."

She paused, then said softly, *"I know I'll get there someday."*

I answered gently: "No, Mom. There's no getting *there*. There's only being here. And I'm glad you're here, and that you trust me enough to share how you feel."

When I returned to my own house, the silence felt heavier than I expected. Alone in that quiet, I found myself grieving both of my stepfathers: tears finally coming in a way I had been holding back.

It was a reminder: love remains, even in the silence.

Grief isn't just endured; it is carried, reshaped, and honored.

Bringing the Journey Full Circle

When I think back to those first days after the loss, I remember moving through thick fog: every step slow, uncertain, heavy. I didn't know then that grief would eventually teach me as much about living as it did about loss.

Along the way, I learned that healing isn't a straight path. It's a series of small choices: to show up, to feel what you feel, to ask for help, to laugh even when tears sit close behind your eyes.

And now, standing here, I see that the person I've become carries pieces of the ones I lost, not as a burden, but as a thread woven into every part of my life. Their love and presence haven't faded; they've simply changed form, finding new ways to live on through me.

That is the full circle: moving from surviving their absence to living with their presence in a different way. One that still brings warmth, still offers guidance, still reminds me that love, once given, never truly leaves.

And if you're reading these words, you've already begun that circle too.

Reflection: What Do I Want to Carry Forward?

Take a breath. Reflect:

- What do I want to bring with me from this season of grief?

- What no longer serves me in this new chapter?

- How has loss shaped my view of life and love?

- What does rebuilding mean to me now?

Final Closing Thought

The journey doesn't end here. It continues, in the way you live, love, and remember.

Grief may have changed you. But it hasn't broken you.

You're still here. Still loving. Still becoming. And your life, though shaped by loss, is still rich with meaning, possibility, and love.

You have walked through fire, and you are still standing.

That is your proof: you are already holding without breaking.

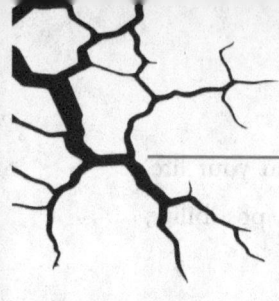

Bonus Chapter
Anchors for the Road Ahead: The Four Pillars That Hold You Steady

"Supporting a grieving parent doesn't mean losing yourself in the process. It means learning how to stand beside them—without disappearing."

T hroughout this journey, we've walked together through the terrain of grief: the shockwaves, the hidden cries, the practical chaos, the quiet resilience.

You'll recognize these Four Pillars from earlier chapters of this book. I've lived them, and we've explored their depth together. Here, I've gathered them in one place—practical steps you can revisit anytime you need steady ground.

These aren't rules. They're anchors—gentle but firm truths to help you steady yourself when the waves rise again.

Pillar One: Resist the Urge to Over-Function

When someone you love is shattered, the instinct is to fix, to carry, to shield. But doing everything for your parent can erase your own needs—and quietly strip them of the chance to rediscover their strength.

In those first months, I threw myself into every detail—calls, forms, bills—believing motion would protect us both. One afternoon, surrounded by stacks of insurance papers and policy terms that felt like another language, I realized I was moving faster than understanding.

So, I slowed down.

I started leading with curiosity instead of urgency—asking every question I could until the next step made sense. I learned that grief doesn't demand quick action; it asks for steady understanding. When I stopped rushing, clarity—and calm—followed.

Later, when my mother looked up from her Queen Chair and said softly, "Let me do this part. I need to know I can still stand," I understood that lesson on a deeper level. Over-functioning had been my armor, but it had also been my way of avoiding my own ache.

Resisting that urge became an act of love—for her and for myself.

Because sometimes the most powerful thing you can do is

pause long enough to ask, What really needs my hand—and what only needs my heart?

Try This:

> Pause before stepping in. Ask, "Do you want me to handle this, or would you like to try first?"

Pillar Two: Set Loving Boundaries

Grief stretches emotions thin—yours and theirs. And when you're the "steady one," people often assume your strength is endless.

It's not.

After my stepfather passed, the phone never stopped ringing. Family, insurance agents, lawyers, church members—everyone meant well. I was managing documents, coordinating appointments, updating siblings, and helping my mother navigate her days. Somewhere in the blur, I forgot I had limits.

When you're the responsible one, you start to mistake availability for love. But being constantly available isn't sustainable—it's slow erosion. You can't pour from an empty cup, and you shouldn't be expected to.

One night, while sitting across from my mom at the kitchen table, I caught myself nodding through fatigue I could barely hide. My body was present, but my spirit was slipping. I took a deep breath and said gently, *"Mom, can we finish this tomorrow?* I want to give you my full attention, but I need a moment to rest."

She looked at me, surprised—and then nodded. That small pause became a turning point. It reminded me that love can have edges, and those edges protect connection rather than distance it.

Boundaries don't block care. They preserve it. They remind you—and everyone else—that you are human.

Try This:

> Before you answer a call or say yes to a request, ask: *"Do I have the capacity to show up fully for this right now?"*
> If the answer is no, that's okay. You're honoring love, not withholding it.

Sample Script:

> "Mom, I want to give you my full attention for this conversation. Can we set aside 30 minutes after dinner so I can be present without rushing?"

Boundaries are not barriers. They are bridges that allow connection to flow without depletion.

Pillar Three: Honor Your Own Grief

It's easy to forget that while you're supporting a grieving parent, you're grieving too.

I remember nights when I'd crawl into bed exhausted from handling the day's details — phone calls, appointments, meals, reminders — only to realize I hadn't taken a moment to acknowledge my own ache. I had been holding space for everyone else, leaving no room for myself.

After my stepfather's death, I tried to stay strong for my mother. I told myself there would be time to feel later. But later never came — only more paperwork, more planning, more quiet. Until one night, I opened his old bowling jersey that still smelled faintly of his cologne. I pressed it to my face and finally cried.

That moment didn't make me weak. It made me real.

Your grief doesn't disappear just because someone else's feels louder. It runs alongside theirs — not competing, not diminishing, just existing in its own language.

There's a silent danger in burying your pain beneath purpose.

If you keep pushing it down, it will find its way out — through irritability, fatigue, or numbness. But when you give it a name, when you allow it a voice, it begins to move.

Sometimes honoring your grief looks quiet: sitting with a cup of tea and letting the tears come without apology. Other times, it looks active: writing, walking, creating space where your emotions can land.

You don't have to choose between being the helper and being human. You can be both.

Try This:

> Create a ritual of your own—a candle lit, a song played, a dish cooked in their honor.

Sample Script (to yourself):

> *"It's okay that I still hurt.* My grief deserves space. I don't have to minimize it to love my parent well."

Your parent's healing matters deeply — but so does your own. When you give yourself permission to grieve, you teach them by example that healing isn't something to rush. It's something to honor.

Pillar Four: Navigate the Practical with Compassion

The paperwork, the estate documents, the insurance policies — they don't wait for grief to ease. Each form, call, and signature arrives heavy with meaning, asking you to make decisions while your heart is still raw.

In the first months after my stepfather's passing, I found myself sitting at the kitchen table surrounded by documents. Policies. Payout forms. Statements that felt more like reminders than records. I wanted to get through them quickly, to finish, to make order out of loss.

But what I learned was this: it's better to lead with *curiosity* than urgency.

When it comes to navigating finances, insurance, or home repairs, take the time to *ask questions until you understand.* Slow down. Make notes. Don't let anyone rush you — not the bank, not the advisor, not even your own sense of pressure to "get it done."

Each signature holds weight. Every policy tells a story. And you deserve the space to read between the lines.

Over time, I developed a rhythm that balanced care with practicality. I attended financial planning meetings with my mother, reviewed paperwork carefully, scanned documents, researched unfamiliar terms, and asked for clarification until things made sense.

That process became its own kind of ministry — a way of honoring her stability and my own learning. Together, we made decisions not from fear, but from understanding.

The truth is, every logistical task carries an emotional undercurrent. A car title isn't just a transfer; it's a farewell. A bill isn't just a payment; it's a continuation of what someone once handled with care.

Approach each step with patience. Lead with questions, not conclusions.

And when confusion rises, remind yourself: this isn't just paperwork. It's part of the healing.

Tips for Navigating the Unknown:

⇒ **Make Lists:** Write down tasks, but circle only what must happen this week.

⇒ **Do It Together:** Sit with your parent during calls, even if they don't say much.

⇒ **Build Breaks In:** After an hour of paperwork, step outside and breathe.

⇒ **Delegate Wisely:** "I'll handle Social Security, but could you take utilities? Sharing the load will help us all breathe."

Move gently. The task is never just a task. It's grief in disguise.

The Road Beyond Survival

Looking back, I see how these Four Pillars became lifelines. They steadied me when I wanted to over-function, protected me when boundaries felt selfish, honored my grief when it tried to disappear, and carried me through the practical without forgetting the humanity underneath.

At first, it felt like survival—day to day, task to task. But slowly, the rhythm shifted. We weren't just reacting to loss anymore; we were living alongside it.

That is the heart of resilient support: not erasing what happened, but integrating it into the life that still awaits you.

A Closing Blessing

May you walk forward with a heart that remembers and a spirit that dares to hope.
May the love you carry be a light in the spaces that feel dark.
May you find joy that honors the ones you've lost, and

courage that carries you into the life still unfolding.
And may you always know—you are not walking this road
alone.

Revisiting the Pillars: Carrying Them With You

Pause. Place your hand over your heart. Then ask yourself:

- Where do I see their love still alive in my daily life?

- What new joys, however small, am I ready to let in—
  without guilt, without apology?

- How has grief changed the way I show up for love—
  with my parent and with myself?

- In what ways can I carry their presence forward—
  through rituals, stories, or the life I'm still shaping?

These aren't answers to finish the story. They are invitations to
live it.

Closing Note

These Four Pillars are here for you whenever you need them. Return to this chapter when the waves rise again.

Let it be a place of grounding, a reminder that you can hold your parent's grief and your own, without losing yourself in the process.

Conclusion

If what you've read has stirred reflections, questions, or memories, know this: you don't have to capture them all now. Healing unfolds in its own rhythm—slow, sacred, and uniquely yours.

You have walked with me through loss, love, and the quiet work of holding without breaking. If you've seen your own story in these pages, let that recognition be your reminder: you are not alone in this journey.

When you're ready, you'll find a companion journal with expanded prompts and practices to help you go deeper—into your own becoming, boundaries, and healing.

You can find it, along with other supporting materials, by visiting mischerekyles.com. But even without it, trust this: you already carry within you everything you need to keep walking forward.

Take what has spoken to your heart. Leave what doesn't fit right now.

Return whenever the waves rise again.

Trust that love, once given, never leaves—it only changes form.

It lives in the memories you keep, the boundaries you honor, and the new life you continue to build.

With you—always in the journey,

Mischere V. Kyles

Epilogue

Grief does not end. It softens. It shifts. It weaves itself into the fabric of your becoming.
And so does love.

If you've walked this far with me, you already know the truth: you are still standing.
You have carried memories, wrestled with silence, and faced roles you never asked for.
And still—you are here.

That is proof enough.

The proof of your love for the one you lost.
The proof of your love for the parent who remains.
The proof of your love for yourself, even when it felt fragile.

Rebuilding has never been about keeping everything intact.

It has always been about discovering that you could bend without shattering—that you could carry both grief and joy, absence and presence, memory and possibility.

And here's the truth: you will break.
There will be nights when the silence feels unbearable,

when the weight of loss presses so deeply you wonder if you'll rise again.

But breaking is not the end.
Breaking is how the heart makes space to restore.
You don't have to let go... you only have to let in.
Let in the love. The memory. The breath of today.

Because even in the breaking, you are being remade.

The journey ahead will not be perfect. Some days will feel
heavy. Others will surprise you with lightness. Both belong.

And when you wonder if you're doing it right, remember this:

You are still here.
You are still becoming.
You are still loving.

And that is the quiet proof of love.

Notes & References

The following works, quotes, and insights helped shape the heart and research foundation of Holding Without Breaking: How to Help Your Grieving Parent Without Losing Yourself.

Each is cited in gratitude and acknowledgment of the wisdom that continues to guide conversations around grief, resilience, and healing.

Epigraphs & Quoted Works

- "What is grief, if not love persevering?" — *WandaVision* (Marvel Studios, 2021).

- Megan Devine, *It's OK That You're Not OK: Meeting Grief and Loss in a Culture That Doesn't Understand* (Sounds True, 2017).

- Kenneth J. Doka, *Grief Is a Journey: Finding Your Path Through Loss* (Atria Books, 2016).

- Pauline Boss, *Ambiguous Loss: Learning to Live with Unresolved Grief* (Harvard University Press, 1999).

- Pauline Boss, *The Myth of Closure: Ambiguous Loss in a Time of Pandemic and Change* (W.W. Norton, 2021).

- Nedra Glover Tawwab, *Set Boundaries, Find Peace: A Guide to Reclaiming Yourself* (TarcherPerigee, 2021).

- George A. Bonanno, *The Other Side of Sadness: What the New Science of Bereavement Tells Us About Life After Loss* (Basic Books, 2009).

- Elisabeth Kübler-Ross and David Kessler, *On Grief and Grieving:*

Finding the Meaning of Grief Through the Five Stages of Loss (Scribner, 2005).

- David Kessler, *Finding Meaning: The Sixth Stage of Grief* (Scribner, 2019).

- William Worden, *Grief Counseling and Grief Therapy: A Handbook for the Mental Health Practitioner* (Springer Publishing, 2018).

- Jamie Anderson, "Grief is just love with no place to go." (Widely attributed quote, origin unknown).

Research & Supporting Insights

Portions of this book were also informed by work in:

- Psychology of resilience and post-loss adaptation (Bonanno, 2009; Stroebe & Schut, 1999, The Dual Process Model of Coping with Bereavement).

- Family systems theory as applied to loss (Bowen, 1978, Family Therapy in Clinical Practice).

- Culturally adaptive grief practices (Doka & Martin, 2010, Grieving Beyond Gender).

Personal Reflections & Narratives

All personal stories, family experiences, and conversations shared throughout this book are drawn from the lived experiences of the author, Mischere V. Kyles, and are recounted with care and permission where appropriate. Names, locations, and identifying details may have been altered to preserve privacy.

Acknowledgment of Influence

My gratitude extends to the grief educators, therapists, spiritual leaders, and readers whose work continues to expand our collective understanding of loss, healing, and legacy.

Your research, empathy, and courage remind us that love, once given, never disappears, it only changes form.

For Companion Resources

To continue your reflection journey, explore:

🕊 *The Holding Without Breaking Companion Journal* — with guided prompts, boundary practices, and resilience-building exercises.

🕊 Additional grief and legacy resources available at www.mischerekyles.com.

Lineage & Legacy Publishing
A division of **Vasiti Enterprises, LLC**

© 2025 Mischere V. Kyles. All Rights Reserved.

No part of this book may be reproduced, distributed, or transmitted in any form without written permission from the publisher.

www.ingramcontent.com/pod-product-compliance
Lightning Source LLC
Chambersburg PA
CBHW010938120626
46554CB00008B/2525